TEACHING YOUR CHILDREN HEALTHY SEXUALITY

JIM BURNS

TEACHING YOUR CHILDREN HEALTHY SEXUALITY

A BIBLICAL APPROACH TO PREPARE THEM FOR LIFE

BETHANYHOUSE
PUBLISHERS

© 2008 by Jim Burns

Published by Bethany House Publishers
11400 Hampshire Avenue South
Bloomington, Minnesota 55438

Bethany House Publishers is a division of
Baker Publishing Group, Grand Rapids, Michigan.

Printed in the United States of America

Library of Congress Cataloging-in-Publication Data

Burns, Jim.
   Teaching your children healthy sexuality : a biblical approach to prepare them for life / Jim Burns.
      p. cm.
   Summary: "Experienced family authority Jim Burns provides a simple and practical guide for parents to help their children develop a healthy and biblical perspective regarding their bodies and sexuality"—Provided by publisher.
   ISBN 978-0-7642-0208-7 (pbk. : alk. paper).
   1. Sex—Religious aspects—Christianity. 2. Sex instruction for children. I. Title.
BT708.B883   2008
248.8'45—dc22   2008003422

Cover design by Lookout Design, Inc.

16 17 18 19 20 21 22   13 12 11 10 9 8 7

In keeping with biblical principles of creation stewardship, Baker Publishing Group advocates the responsible use of our natural resources. As a member of the Green Press Initiative, our company uses recycled paper when possible. The text paper of this book is composed in part of post-consumer waste.

Books by Jim Burns

Addicted to God

Building Blocks for a Solid Family

Closer (with Cathy Burns)

*Confident Parenting**

*Creating an Intimate Marriage**

Faith Conversations for Families

One Life

*Partnering With Parents in Youth Ministry***

Teenology

Tough Problems, Real Solutions

PURE FOUNDATIONS

Accept Nothing Less

God Made Your Body

How God Makes Babies

The Purity Code

Teaching Your Children Healthy Sexuality†

* Audio CD; DVD & Curriculum Kit also available

† Parents' Kit also available: *The Purity Code, Teaching Your Children Healthy Sexuality,* and Audio Resource CD

**With Mike DeVries

To Jon Wallace

*You are a friend closer than a brother. You have left your footprints
on my heart, and I will never, ever be the same.
Thank you for your leadership, friendship, integrity, and
fully committed life. You inspire me!*

Thank you . . .

Cindy Ward . . . for your incredible partnership in ministry. You make a difference every day in the lives of people. You live out your faith and values as strongly as anyone I have ever known. Thank you for being such an inspiration.

Bill Bauer . . . for the wisdom you bring and the generosity you share.

Randy Bramel, Terry Hartshorn, Tom Purcell, and Bucky Oltmans . . . Tuesday mornings are always a highlight of the week.

The HomeWord Staff . . . Your dedication is nothing short of miraculous, plus you make HomeWord a fun place to spend several hours a day. Thank you to Aubrey Ashford, Bill Bauer, Dean Bruns, Ben Camp, Emily De La Torre, Rosalie De Santis, Lindsey DeVito, Ted Evans, Brent Ferguson, Dave Hamilton, Betty Harper, Judy Hedgren, Kendall Hops, Kathy Kappauf, Jim Liebelt, Roger Marsh, Linda McKinley, Megan Michaelson,

Mary Perdue, Andrea Popkes, Susan Rettino, Wayne Rice, Scott Singletary, Melinda Sylstra, Ann Trotter, and Derek Yankoff.

Howard and Roberta Ahmanson . . . the dream for an entire PURE FOUNDATIONS campaign was birthed at the Willard Hotel in Washington, D. C., with you. Thank you so much for all you do to make a difference. God bless you.

The HomeWord Board . . . There is not a more generous and encouraging board in the universe. Thank you to Jeff Armour, Steve Arterburn, Randy Bramel, Susan Bramel, Todd Dean, Pam Emery, Rod Emery, Rick Haugen, Bob Howard, David Lane, Kelly Mitchell, Geoff Moore, Lucie Moore, Gordon Schaller, and Jon Wallace.

Cathy Burns . . . Your sacrificial love, commitment, and partnership in helping this generation of parents and kids not settle for mediocrity is nothing short of miraculous. I am grateful you said yes.

Christy, Rebecca, and Heidi . . . my daughters are the delight of my life.

Virginia . . . Dad called you his angel and he was so right.

Special thanks to my dad for everything! Dad passed into eternity during the writing of this book. I am a deeply grateful son.

I am a man most blessed.

Contents

CHAPTER ONE

Teaching Your Kids Value-Centered Sexuality

"How many of you received healthy, value-centered sex education from your parents growing up?" It's a question I ask parents everywhere. And the response is always the same. In a gathering of, say, four hundred people, usually four will raise their hands. It doesn't matter where I am—speaking in a church or another place—the ratio is consistent.

It's true: Our parents didn't talk to us about healthy sexuality, and, unfortunately, we're not doing much better with own children. A vast majority of young people say they receive more information about sexuality from their friends, media, and school than from their own home. *This is not good news, especially when all studies show that the more positive, value-centered sex education kids receive in their home, the less promiscuous they will be.*

A parent is almost always the person who has the best interest of their child in mind when it comes to sexuality. And you and I have the opportunity to provide our children healthy, *value-centered* sex education that is based on what God values. He has given us our sexuality. In the framework of Scripture, sex is not dirty. In the context of marriage it is rather beautiful. The world's culture has cheapened sex, but God's view of sexuality is wonderful and magnificent.

Frankly, it's not the primary job of schools to teach morals and values, and it definitely shouldn't be left to the latest rock star or media magnate. And friends? I now laugh out loud at what my friends told me in the fifth grade about the birds and the bees. Talk about wrong and misguided information.

Even though this generation of parents typically wants to do a better job of communication, too many well-meaning moms and dads are remaining silent for too long. Most didn't have a healthy conversation about sexuality modeled for them. They are afraid that talking about "it" will rob their children of their sexual innocence, or their children's sexual desires might be awakened early. Some parents avoid bringing up the subject because they might be asked about their experiences, and they aren't all that proud of how they handled their own sexuality. Regardless, the best person to teach your children about sexuality and relationships is you!

The Goal: A Lifetime of Sexual Integrity

For many parents, the foremost goal is to do everything possible to make sure their child stays pure until his or her wedding day. This is wonderful, but I believe we can and should do much more for our children. We can help establish in them lasting sexual integrity that starts at a young age and extends throughout their entire life, guiding their self-image, how they treat members of the opposite sex, and how they view and enjoy intimacy in marriage, as well as how resolute they are to remain faithful in mind and body. I compare it to teaching our children healthy eating habits. We certainly want them to eat their broccoli, whole grain breads, and other good things while living at home, but more than anything, we want them to continue reaping and enjoying the benefits of eating healthy after they have moved out.

This kind of a core belief in sexual integrity doesn't come from a one-time conversation or a sex education class. It develops as parents instruct, dialogue, and model a life of value-centered sexuality. When I talk with young people who have grown up with sexual integrity, they almost always mention having ongoing conversations with their parents that at least most of the time felt very natural. No matter what the age, kids learn best when they talk and dialogue, not just when parents lecture.

Scott and Anne came to me for premarital counseling. They had both previously been in my youth group. During one session we talked about sexuality. I was pleased to hear they were both virgins; this is usually not the case today, even among

Christians. I asked how they had chosen sexual integrity when most of their generation had not. Their answer was insightful. First, they said their parents had talked openly and freely about sex-related issues. Secondly, while in the high school youth group, they had taken a sexual purity pledge very seriously. Thirdly, although they did have a strong sex drive and it had not been easy to wait, they both had made a decision to practice the spiritual discipline of sexual abstinence. Personally, I have found that when young people like Scott and Anne commit to only the physical discipline of sexual abstinence, they do not do as well as those who honor and love God with their eyes, mind, and heart, as well as their body. This all-out commitment to sexual purity is living according to what I call the Purity Code (explained in more detail in chapter 2).

Scott and Anne's wedding was a joyous occasion, and I made it a point to thank both sets of parents for the incredible start they had given the young couple. The parents laughed and said it wasn't always easy. In fact, they said some conversations were downright uncomfortable. But the results were well worth the discomfort. And Scott and Anne were on their way to discovering what authorities have known for years: Sex is better in marriage. Sex is better when couples have a spiritual connection, and sex is not better if you live together before marriage.[1]

You may be wondering, *what does this story have to do with me and my family? My kids are still young.* Actually, the very best time to introduce healthy sexuality is when children are young. Then you can naturally teach healthy values at the proper developmental stage of life.

What Our Kids Are Facing

To do the very best job we can as parents, we need to become students of the culture in which our kids are growing up. These days, that culture is "aging" kids as never before. We may have been teenagers once, but we were never "their age" because they experience so much so young. What today's ten-year-olds face is vastly different from what we dealt with at age ten.

I realize that parents of younger children may feel like skipping some of the culture-related information here that tends to look at the teenage years, but don't do it. Your time is right around the corner.

Here are the facts, and they aren't pretty. Without setting a solid foundation of healthy sexuality and without a goal of sexual integrity, your kids can wind up on the wrong side of these statistics.

The Facts[2]

- Nearly 60 percent of sixteen- to eighteen-year-olds have had sexual intercourse.

- Nearly one-third of thirteen- to fifteen-year-olds have had sexual intercourse.

- Nearly 60 percent of sexually active teenagers do not use any method of birth control, and the same number of kids has never once talked with their parents about birth control.

- Ninety percent of kids surveyed believe in marriage, yet 74 percent say they would live with someone before or instead of marriage.

- Thirty-one percent of teen girl virgins say they have felt pressured by a guy to go further.

- Sixty-seven percent of teens who have had intercourse wish they had waited.

- Over half of the young people in America claim to have had oral sex by the age of twenty-two.

- The average age of the first Internet exposure to pornography is eleven years old.

- Three million new cases of sexually transmitted diseases (STDs) occur each year among teenagers.

- In the summer of 2000, *Twist* magazine did an online survey of ten thousand girls, over half of whom were under fourteen. Amazingly, 24 percent of the girls who said they were virgins responded that they engaged in oral sex.

- There are fourteen thousand acts of intercourse or sexual innuendo each year on primetime TV.

These statistics are especially alarming when you consider that behind the numbers are names and faces and families and stories. No, not every story can be changed by teaching healthy sexuality, but many can change. Kids today aren't just looking for the "birds and bees" talk. They want answers, and I think the best place to get those answers is from their parents.

For a look at what kids are facing, I thought you'd be interested in knowing some of the questions I get from young Christians.

- How far is too far?

- Is it possible to get the Pill without my parents' knowledge?

- I stumbled upon some pornography on the Internet. Now I can't help myself and I go to sites every day. It is affecting my spiritual life and the way I view girls. I think I'm addicted. What can I do to get help?

- How often do married people usually have sexual intercourse?

- Is oral sex okay? If you participate in oral sex, are you still a virgin?

- All of my middle-school girl friends (except me) believe it is okay to have "friends with benefits." They don't want to have sexual intercourse, but hooking up is no big deal. What is your opinion?

- Is masturbation wrong?

- What do you think about girls getting back massages from their boyfriends? Sometimes I think my boyfriend would like to go farther than just the back.

- At what age is a boy's first erection?

- Is it true that you can get STDs without having sexual intercourse?

- I'm afraid of AIDS. What can I do to not get it?

- Will God condemn me if I have premarital sex? Will He forgive me?

- Do you think it is okay for me and my friends to have boy/girl sleepovers as long as there are chaperones?

- What can a guy do if he has a problem of lust toward other guys? How can I handle it without having to be gay?

- Does God forgive Christians who have had abortions?

- I have been sexually abused for five years and haven't told anyone about it. How can I try to forget and deal with it?

The questions are sobering, aren't they? I realize that you may not be feeling very optimistic right now about your child's future, but the fact remains that there is hope and there are answers. Kids today receive a variety of mixed messages when it comes to sexuality, and it's our job to help sort out the messages and their questions.

Mixed Messages

Young people have a great deal of tension about their sexuality and are filled with questions partly because of the conflicting information they receive from different sources. To simplify, let's look at three areas where kids receive mixed messages.

1. Parents say, "Don't do it . . ." (and then nothing else is discussed—silence).
2. The church says, "Don't do it because it is dirty, rotten, and sinful, so save it until you're married!"
3. Secular culture says, "This is how you do it—and make sure you use a condom."

We have already covered the fact that parents seldom take the lead when it comes to presenting healthy sex education with their children. Kids tell me that all they hear from their parents is, "Don't do it," with little or no explanation. Most parents do not take the time to deal with questions like the ones presented earlier. Although I think the church in recent years has done a much better job about communicating a healthy form of sexuality, kids still think they hear from the church that sex is a dirty, sinful thing . . . and that they should wait to experience that dirty, sinful thing when they are married! Maybe that's why many married couples still struggle with enjoying their God-given sexuality. As I mentioned, though, today the church has wonderful resources and is much more open to providing good information. Unfortunately, secular culture is thrilled to give its opinion of sexuality. Movies, TV shows, music, the Web, and many celebrities express attitudes and views that are almost the opposite of the values we want to pass on. We can't expect the secular culture to present morals and healthy values to our kids. It is our job. Silence or complaining doesn't help our kids.

The Crisis

Most authorities believe that this generation of young people is living through a sexual crisis. What is important to understand is that the crisis is perceived differently in society. The secular world presents sexual promiscuity as a crisis based on the *results* of promiscuity: unwed mothers, stretched finances, sexually transmitted diseases, abortions, and so on. The secular community readily admits there is a problem. But again, the focus is on consequences.

The Christian perspective is much more concerned for the whole person. Our focus is on the development of healthy values, being responsible for one's actions, one's relationship with God, and generally what is right and wrong. The Christian perspective deals with, to a greater extent, how we treat members of the opposite sex and our deeper moral character.

In a recent debate I had with a leader in the Planned Parenthood movement, we were able to agree on many issues. We agreed that a majority of kids are experimenting with sexual behavior. We both had a deep concern for unwed mothers and their children. We had a mutual concern about the incidence of sexually transmitted diseases and sexual abuse. We even agreed that parents can provide the best and most effective sex education. What we couldn't agree on was that the core problem lies not just in the results of promiscuity but what feeds into it: declining morals and values, as well as young people trying to avoid responsibility for their sexual behavior.

Another troubling aspect of the crisis is that sex fools kids into "instant intimacy." When young people become physically intimate with each other and then break up, it leaves scars. Over the past decade I have seen this trend in my own ministry with students. A young woman or man would talk to me about a breakup almost like a divorce. The more I saw a negative change in the emotional health of students who had just broken up, the more I heard they had been sexually involved. The story goes like this: "We really loved each other. We didn't mean to get so physically involved, but we slipped. The more time we spent on a sexual level, the closer we got. Now we have broken up and I feel devastated. I'm not sure I can go on." Some experts say that as many as 70 percent of teenage suicide attempts stem from a broken romantic relationship.

All of this is to say that there is no such thing as casual sex. Sexual intimacy affects our emotional, relational, mental, and spiritual life, not to mention our physical well-being.

For parents of younger children, one major concern is what we call the *early sexualization* of children. Today we are finding that early exposure to sexually explicit experiences is causing a rapidly deteriorating sexual mindset with kids. If you have kept your child from watching movies and TV programs with sexual content, good for you. We shouldn't be trying to raise "happy" children who get their way. We are trying to raise *responsible* children who will make wise decisions about their morality. Liberal doses of listening to and viewing sexual content is not healthy.

One of the many jobs of a parent is monitoring the media our kids see and use, as well as their friendships. *We need to become students of their culture. We need to listen to what they listen to, watch what they watch, and read what they read.* I know this may sound contradictory when I previously applauded parents for creating media-safe homes, but let me explain. As kids get older and are exposed to media, it is very important for parents to take the lead in helping their children learn to discern what is healthy and what is not healthy content. Early sexualization is simply not healthy; in today's culture, a parent must become very familiar with youth culture influences, and dialogue is necessary between parents and their children. Kids learn best when they dialogue—not when Mom or Dad lecture.

A very fine Christian school in our area puts on a prom night for middle-schoolers. The parents buy expensive prom-type outfits. Many of the kids eat at wonderful restaurants and arrive in limousines. It is well-chaperoned, and the program is good, clean fun. My problem with the experience is that it gives kids in middle school an amazing date experience that moves them along too fast with the opposite sex. Don't get me wrong—I like the idea of giving our children "markers" when it comes to dating and growing up. I personally think it is better when young people can look forward to a marker in life, like a special prom event later in high school, or driving, or voting. Do not allow the dating marker to creep too early into your child's development. In today's culture, this may be just one of the battles you will have to win. And I do believe that positive peer events help kids learn how to relate in a healthy manner with the opposite sex. That's one of the many reasons why I am a huge proponent of youth and children's ministries in churches. However, to allow kids to experience boy/girl relationships on a deeper level at too young an age can bring on early sexualization and its related problems (which are covered in greater detail in chapter 5).

Some parents see no problem with kids dating younger than sixteen. Frankly, I do. Here's what one study discovered:

Age of Dating	% Who Have Sex Before Graduation[3]
12 years	91%
13 years	56%
14 years	53%
15 years	40%
16 years	20%

Your Job Description

No doubt you wouldn't be reading this book if you didn't have many of the same concerns I do. Some parents, though, look at the sexual revolution and become paralyzed with fear. Complaining about a deteriorating culture won't help our children. We need to face the facts and deal with the issues in a healthy and beneficial way. It won't always be easy or comfortable, but the results will definitely be worth it.

What follows are five key things children need in order to develop a healthy view of their sexuality and a better relationship with their parents. The rest of this book is dedicated to giving you the tools and understanding it takes to accomplish this somewhat daunting task.

1. Talk

Communication is a key to developing healthy sexuality. I'll say it again: Kids learn best when they dialogue rather just hearing lectures from Mom and Dad. Make the teaching of healthy sexual values as normal and natural as possible. Remember that each child is different. One of our children was very open to talking with us about sexual matters. Another was absolutely silent and only later did we understand that she was actually listening. The baby of the family told us she already knew all this stuff because her sisters had taught her long before we thought they should. Nevertheless, developing a healthy atmosphere of conversation about sexuality is critical. Make sure your conversations are developmentally appropriate, and make it a goal to talk about all aspects of sexuality over a period of time. Your ultimate goal is to bring meaning and value to their sexuality that will help them decide to live a life of sexual integrity.

2. Role Models With Honesty and Integrity

Talking about sexuality can be uncomfortable. Some of us didn't handle our hormones as well as we wished when we were young. No matter what our situation, dealing with issues in an honest manner is the healthiest approach. You don't have to share all your "sins of the past," but don't be afraid to say that the reason you have concerns for your children is because you didn't get this kind of healthy conversation, and it affected you. Your own sexual integrity will also play a major factor in bringing security to your children. In fact, one of the great Proverbs in the Bible says, "The man [or woman] of integrity walks securely . . ." (Proverbs 10:9), and I am convinced that the man or woman who lives a life of integrity will have much more secure children as well. Let's face it: You can't ask your kids to live out a way of life that you aren't doing yourself. I remember a recent conversation with a single mom who was concerned about her teenage son being sexually promiscuous. She had brought a parade of men into their home to sleep with her over the past three years. My comment to her in love but firmness was, "You can't expect something from your son if you aren't willing to follow the same values."

3. Positive Peer Influence

People talk so much about negative peer pressure, but there is also such a thing as positive peer influence. Don't underestimate the influence of your children's friends. As they get older, you obviously can't legislate every moment with every friend, but you can do a great deal to bring positive peer influence into the lives of your kids. Church activities, sports, band, and any other healthy activity will help your kids find good friendships. Encourage the good friendships. Go the extra mile to keep friendships healthy. As kids get older, this is sometimes easier said than done, but don't give up. Authorities tell us that kids will take on the values of their friends. Get to know your kids' friends and their families. Cathy and I actually built a pool in our backyard when our kids got older so that our house would be *the* place to hang out. Obviously that is not the answer for everyone, but the point is to make positive peer influence a priority. Just this past summer some very wise parents told me that their middle school daughter was beginning to spend time with the wrong crowd. They invited one of her church friends to go to a Christian summer camp with her and offered to provide scholarship help. The camp brought their daughter back into a better peer group. This was good thinking on the part of the parents.

4. Grace and Forgiveness

As you develop conversations with your children about healthy sexuality, make sure there is plenty of positive talk about grace and forgiveness. God is not a "killjoy" when it comes to our sexuality. He cares about every aspect of our life, including our sexuality. Some families mean well, but in their desperation to teach their kids values, they turn sexuality into something dirty. Don't be one of those parents. Kids need help in setting healthy, positive standards for their sexuality and relationships, and it is always more effective when surrounded with grace and forgiveness. In the next chapter, we will talk about helping our kids build a "theology of sexuality." Sometimes before we teach our children, we need to develop our own theology around the theme that God created our sexuality and sees it as very good in the context of marriage and biblical standards.

5. Something Is Better Than Nothing

There have been times in Cathy's and my life with our own children when we have either been silent for too long or excessively intense. In a world where most kids do not receive much input at all from their parents, never forget the old adage, "Something is better than nothing." It is never too early to begin and never too late to start talking about this most important subject. There will be a few bumps along the way and, who knows, maybe even a few bruises. Some of our dearest friends, who frankly did a lot of what I am suggesting in this book, just found out their teenage daughter is pregnant, but all in all, the fact still remains that the more positive, healthy sexuality taught from home, the less promiscuous children will be.

Teaching your children healthy sexuality is definitely a process, and you will have some uncomfortable moments, but you may also have a few smiles along the way. A close friend of mine told me a story about a dad and his thirteen-year-old son who went on a fishing trip. The other purpose, besides catching fish, was to listen to a wonderful CD together about sexuality, like the one HomeWord offers in our Pure Foundations series. The young man kept quiet as the CD played. In fact, the dad wasn't even sure if he was actually paying attention. After the CD ended, the son just looked out the window. Finally his dad said, "Son, what do you think about all this?"

Hesitantly, the boy said, "I can think of three things:

"One, I can't believe you and Mom actually do that.

"Two, I think it's gross.

"Three, when I get married, I think I'm really going to like it!"

Helping our kids build a theology of healthy sexuality is not as far of a reach as one might think. We can make a difference, and it's not all that difficult. We will look at this topic next.

CHAPTER TWO

Building a Foundation to Teach the Purity Code

I once heard that the average sixteen-year-old boy has a sexual thought every twenty seconds. When I mentioned this to a group of students in North Carolina, I had a young man approach me and ask if he could talk with me privately. "Sure, what's up?" I asked. He smiled and said, "You know that statistic about having a sexual thought every twenty seconds?" I nodded my head, and he continued, "Well, what am I supposed to think about the other nineteen seconds? It's always on my mind!" We both had a good laugh, but his comment was telling. By the time young people get through puberty, they *do* think about sex and relationships—A LOT.

As parents, we deeply desire our children to have a healthy God-given view of their sexuality, and we want them to know that thinking about their sexuality is very common. But if we keep silent about sex or approach the subject with a negative attitude, we send majorly mixed messages to our children. We are the ones who must help them see that everything from their changing bodies to their changing thoughts is normal.

We parents are also in the best position to show our kids how living by the Purity Code is normal, healthy, and God-centered. Later in this chapter I will present more details about the Purity Code, but for now, it's important to know that it is not just about sex and saving yourself for marriage. Students are asked to make this pledge:

"In honor of God, my family, and my future spouse, I commit my life to sexual purity."

It encourages making a *lifetime* commitment to:

- Honoring God with your body
- Renewing your mind for the good
- Turning your eyes from worthless things
- Guarding your heart above all else

This book and other resources in my PURE FOUNDATIONS series are intended to help parents introduce the Purity Code to their children. You will be the one to help build the foundation your kid will need to make this commitment—a foundation of healthy sexuality that is based on Scripture and strong enough to withstand the forces of secular culture.

Cultural Realities

Sex and sexuality are a natural part of our lives and our children's lives because God made us sexual beings. At a certain age, our children's God-given sex drive will kick in. However, there are at least three other factors that we have to look at to help our kids understand how they are being influenced by sex, even at a young age.

No matter how hard you try, you will not be able to keep your kids in a bubble long enough to not be influenced or impacted by the culture's view of sex. In fact, many studies tell us that if kids have a repressed view of sex, it can be quite unhealthy. This doesn't mean we buy in to the culture's sexual revolution, but the best sex education is honest and I believe comes from a biblical foundation, so we have to help our children understand how and why sex influences their lives.

Sex is everywhere in the culture. You can't drive past billboards, watch TV, listen to the radio, read a magazine, or basically have a conversation without realizing that we live in a sexual culture. Sex sells and everyone knows it.

I remember a time when Cathy and I were driving our three girls to see Grandma and Grandpa. We live at the beach in Southern California, so we chose to drive the Pacific Coast Highway. It's a beautiful drive, though it has a plethora of billboards selling anything from suntan lotion to cars. Most billboards seem to feature a beautiful woman wearing less clothing than would seem appropriate. This particular day a billboard caught my attention somewhere between Newport Beach and

Huntington Beach. It showed the bare back of a shapely blonde looking over her shoulder, seemingly staring at me as I drove by in our minivan. The sign read "Drink Tequila," and then it named the brand. There is alcoholism in my extended family system, and because I believe there is a biological predisposition to alcoholism, I don't drink. However, because of the sign (or rather the photo of the woman), I can still recall the brand name of the tequila!

Examples of sexual images or references around us are endless. Just recently I asked a group of preteens and teens to break into groups and, in two minutes, list as many popular songs with sexual innuendos as they could. The "losing" group came up with almost twenty songs.

If we are going to help our children build a foundation of healthy beliefs related to sexuality, we need to acknowledge that kids will think about sex, because it's everywhere in the culture. Your job will be to teach your children how to discern what is a good message or a bad message. For example, we have a rule in the Burns home that I listen to all the new music that comes into the house. Lately, that feels somewhat like a full-time job. My kids will say they don't notice or care about the lyrics. That's fine. Then it's my job to help them listen to the words and see if messages are healthy or unhealthy. That's our job with every form of media and even conversations (see chapter 3 and the discussion about modesty). How will our children learn to discern if we don't teach them how?

Sex is mysterious. It almost doesn't seem possible in today's sex-filled world, but sex is still mysterious, which is another reason why kids will think about it. A long time ago there was a TV commercial about a financial investment company. When two people started to talk about making money, everyone around them suddenly quieted down to listen in. The tagline was simple: "When E. F. Hutton talks, people listen."

The effect is even more so when people are discussing sexuality. Cathy and I were at the beach one day with our friends, Steve and Andrea, enjoying the sun and the surf. In the afternoon, eight teenage girls placed their beach towels nearby. Their conversation quickly turned into a direct and open talk about sex. All of a sudden I realized that none of us adults was talking. Because we had teenagers, we were all listening in on the girls' conversation.

Sex influences our kids because it is mysterious and, like us, they are naturally curious. They are going to ask questions. They are going to talk about it. So where would you rather have them get their information? From you, from some misinformed fifth graders, or from someone else entirely who has unhealthy morals and values? That's why we need to demystify sexuality and be the ones to help them build a solid foundation of healthy views about sex and relationships. Just acknowledge to them that sex is mysterious and that you are willing to discuss any subject in a nonjudgmental way at any time.

I still remember the day one of our daughters at age ten asked me, "Daddy, what is oral sex?" My first reaction was to rail on the national news, which had been making it a headline because of the Monica Lewinsky/President Clinton scandal. And now my innocent daughter was asking an innocent question.

So I told her to ask her mother! Just kidding. Although that's what I wanted to do, I tried my best to give her an answer that was developmentally appropriate for the mind of a ten-year-old. She didn't need all the details, she just needed the basics at that time. My goal was to not make her feel embarrassed or ashamed for asking a question like that.

If you face a similar situation, especially when a question catches you by surprise, it's more than okay to say something like, "That is a very important question, and Mommy and I will talk with you about it after dinner tonight." Then (if you are married) get together with your spouse and decide how you are going to discuss an honest question like this with your children. When you acknowledge with your children that sex is mysterious—that it's natural to wonder about it—it will help relieve any tension they might have about the subject.

Sex is enjoyable! Some parents have a hard time at first believing this is a good message for young people to hear, but we do need to help our children learn that sex is enjoyable, and under the right situation it is a beautiful response to a loving marriage.

Cathy and I have tried to teach our girls the biblical standards for sexuality and, at the same time, we have told them that sex is a very enjoyable experience within the right context. Just because you tell your kids that sex is fun doesn't mean it will cause them to experiment. Truth is always the better teacher. I believe that when you tell your kids the truth, it will create a trusting relationship that will only enhance their desire to live with moral purity. At the same time, they also need to know that sex is not always enjoyable. In the chapters on sexual abuse and sexually transmitted diseases, I will deal with the painful issues of the trauma of being violated and the exposure to health risks with promiscuous sex. However, as we teach our kids to view their sexuality in a positive manner, it will typically move them toward the self-discipline to wait.

A Theology of Healthy Sexuality

When it comes to laying a moral foundation for sexuality integrity and the Purity Code, I am always amazed at how much the Bible deals with this subject. Unfortunately, I think most young people have a warped view of sexuality. It's a mix between what they have learned from an immoral culture (or an amoral culture, at best) and the silence or negativity of their parents. I believe it is our job to teach what the Bible says about sex and relationships. More could be written on this subject, but let me provide for you a framework of what I would want to get across to my own children and yours.

God Created Sex

The Lord God said, "It is not good for the man to be alone. I will make a helper suitable for him." Now the Lord God had formed out of the ground all the beasts of the field and all the birds of the air. He brought them to the man to see what he would name them; and whatever the man called each living creature, that was its name. So the man gave names to all the livestock, the birds of the air and all the beasts of the field. But for Adam no suitable helper was found. So the Lord God caused the man to fall into a deep sleep; and while he was sleeping, he took one of the man's ribs and closed up the place with flesh. Then the Lord God made a woman from the rib he had taken out of the man, and he brought her to the man. The man said, "This is now bone of my bones and flesh of my flesh; she shall be called 'woman,' for she was taken out of man." For this reason a man will leave his father and mother and be united to his wife, and they will become one flesh. The man and his wife were both naked, and they felt no shame.

Genesis 2:18–25

God created male and female. Since He created man and woman, He also created our sexuality. Kids need to know that sexuality is God's idea. Because God created our sexuality, we will want to honor Him with our bodies. Sex is God's idea, and we have to set the standards high.

God Sees Sex as "Very Good"

Then God said, "Let us make man in our image, in our likeness, and let them rule over the fish of the sea and the birds of the air, over the livestock, over all the earth, and over all the creatures that move along the ground." . . . God saw all that he had made, and it was very good. And there was evening, and there was morning—the sixth day.

Genesis 1:26, 31

Not only did God create our sexuality, but He sees it as "very good." The creation account in the Bible gives an explanation of all that God created. Everything He created is described, and it always ends with these words: "and it was good." When God created male and female, the Scripture says, "Then God said . . . 'it was *very* good'" (emphasis mine). Obviously, this Scripture is talking about much more than our sexuality, but it does include our sexuality. Far too many young people (and some of us older ones too) have a warped view of God's creation of the beauty of male and female and all that entails. Parents must help their children have a proper understanding of God's creation, including learning to accept their sexuality as a gift from God. As with any gift from God, we need to teach them how to ensure that the gift is set apart and sanctified. We have to lay the groundwork for developing a foundation for healthy sexuality that includes helping kids understand the precious gift they have been given and using it in the right context.

The Bible on Adultery

> *You shall not commit adultery.*
>
> Exodus 20:14

We need to teach our children about the immorality of adultery—when two people have sexual intercourse and at least one of them is married to someone else. God's grace abounds, but there are consequences to these actions. We have to teach our children that the reason God puts commandments like this in the Bible, including this one from the Ten Commandments, is because He wants the best for us. God is not a killjoy when it comes to sexuality. He is looking out for the moral, spiritual, and relational well-being of each and every person by instructing, "Don't commit adultery."

Even outside the biblical context, secular social science has proven that adultery tears apart relationships. It does nothing to bring a husband and wife and their family together; rather, it breaks them apart. Is healing possible if someone breaks this commandment? Of course it is. But the process is often a slow and slippery adventure. Frankly, without the forgiveness and strength of God, it is very difficult for a couple and family to come back together after an affair. It is also important that our children understand the pain of emotional affairs too. (More on this in chapter 7.)

The Bible on Fornication

> *It is God's will that you should be sanctified: that you should avoid sexual immorality.*
>
> 1 Thessalonians 4:3

The Greek word in the Scripture above is *pornea,* and it literally means "immorality." In some versions of the Bible, the word is translated as "fornication." Fornication, of course, is when two people have a sexual relationship and they are not married. It is interesting to note that the word *pornography* has the same root word as well. We not only have to teach our children to "avoid immorality," but we have to teach them *how* to avoid it. (See chapter 3 on setting standards.) As we help build this foundation for our kids from hopefully a young age, this Scripture goes on to say "that each of you should learn to control his [or her] own body." It is one thing to tell our kids, "Don't do it!" The higher calling is to teach them why and how to remain sexually pure. I don't believe fornication relates just to sexual intercourse. One of the mistakes some parents and some churches make is they put the total emphasis on not having sexual intercourse, when in reality the greater goal is to teach our kids sexual integrity.

The Bible on the Union Between Man and Wife: One Flesh

"Haven't you read," he replied, "that at the beginning the Creator 'made them male and female,' and said, 'For this reason a man will leave his father and mother and be united to his wife, and the two will become one flesh'? So they are no longer two, but one. Therefore what God has joined together, let man not separate."

Matthew 19:4–6

This is another powerful concept from the mouth of Jesus that we must teach our children. Jesus is quoting the Old Testament creation account as He talks about a man and woman becoming one flesh. In sexual intercourse (and this Scripture is referring to more than just sexual intercourse), it is a perfect example of two literally being joined together to become one flesh. Because of the media and other avenues that promote "free love," people have a belief that there is something called casual sex. There is no such thing as casual sex. You can't be physically joined together and call that casual. My good friends and marriage experts, Gary and Barb Rosberg, put it this way: "We can never experience truly satisfying and fulfilling sex apart from relationship."[1] They are so right.

A growing popular phrase on college campuses as well as middle and high school campuses is "friends with benefits." This refers to people being in a casual sexual relationship without the commitment of marriage to each other. This kind of thinking can be extremely dangerous to relationships. Ultimately, the less baggage our kids bring into their own marriages, the better off they will be. When a couple waits to become one flesh on their wedding night for the first time, the odds go up greatly that their marriage will thrive and even that their sexual experience throughout the marriage will be more fulfilling.

Years ago I read an interesting book by a sociologist from the University of Wisconsin, Ray Short, entitled *Sex, Love, or Infatuation: How Can I Really Know?* He wrote in a chapter entitled, "To Be or Not to Be a Virgin," that "science has established nine facts concerning the probable effect of premarital sex on your marriage."[2] These facts, listed below, are the kind of facts I share with kids before they would ever consider becoming "one flesh" prior to marriage. They don't keep the hormones from raging, but they are very good, logical thoughts on waiting until marriage for sex.

- Fact 1: Premarital sex tends to break up couples.

- Fact 2: Many men do not want to marry a woman who has had intercourse with someone else.

- Fact 3: Those who have premarital sex tend to have less happy marriages.

- Fact 4: Those who have premarital sex are more likely to have their marriage end in divorce.

- Fact 5: Persons and couples who have had premarital sex are more likely to have extramarital affairs as well.

- Fact 6: Having premarital sex may fool you into marrying a person who is not right for you.

- Fact 7: Persons and couples who have premarital sex experience sexual satisfaction sooner after they are married. HOWEVER—

- Fact 8: They are likely to be less satisfied overall with their sex life during marriage.

- Fact 9: Poor premarital sexual habits can be carried over to spoil sex in marriage.[3]

The Bible on the Human Body

Flee from sexual immorality. All other sins a man commits are outside his body, but he who sins sexually sins against his own body. Do you not know that your body is a temple of the Holy Spirit, who is in you, whom you have received from God? You are not your own; you were bought at a price. Therefore honor God with your body.

1 Corinthians 6:18–20

This is one of the finest "sermonettes" on being sexually pure I have ever seen. When our own children were getting to the place where we would help them consider the concept of sexual purity and integrity, this was the Scripture that we shared with them. It's a message of what and how to be sexually pure with a challenge at the end: honor God with your body.

Flee from sexual immorality. All other sins a man commits are outside his body, but he (or she) who sins sexually sins against their own body. (v. 18)

There is that word again—*pornea*, or immorality. The concept here is that sexual immorality misses the mark of God's standards on sexuality. Our task is to teach our kids to flee from it because it's the right and pure thing to do. This Scripture also teaches us that there are consequences to sexual sin, and sometimes those consequences are to our own body. The nearly three million new cases of STDs among young people each year is just one example.

One story I have shared with my children involves someone who had been in my youth group. Jeanne went on to be in a sorority at UCLA. She was one of the most beautiful young women I have ever known, on the inside and outside. During one Christmas break, she told me about an encounter she had had with her sorority sisters. During the semester they had been teasing her about being a virgin. Most seemed to think she was the only virgin in this particular sorority. At one all-sorority dinner it came to a head when the girls again mocked her and called her "Virgin Jeanne." Finally she had had enough and she pushed back, saying through her tears, "Any day I could become like you, but none of you could ever bring your virginity back!" The girls were silenced with that comment. Jeanne later told me that many of the girls came to her quietly and alone and told her they now wished that they had waited. We must help our kids flee from sexual immortality and move toward sexual integrity.

Do you not know that your body is a temple of the Holy Spirit who is in you, whom you have received from God? (v. 19)

This concept of our bodies being the temple of God has been missed by younger generations. It truly is a beautiful illustration of the Spirit of God taking up residency in the body of a believer. Our bodies are so much more than skin, bones, tissue, and organs. Literally, the Spirit of the living God resides in us, and the foundation we are to lay out for our children and ourselves is that of radically respecting our body as well as the bodies of others. Sexuality is only one aspect of how we are to respect our bodies.

Radical respect teaches our kids that the opposite sex

possesses the Spirit of God in them. We are called to honor them and treat them with the same value and respect that God treats them with. As my own girls got old enough to understand, I challenged them to look at the opposite sex not from a sexy, worldly view but rather to treat them as brothers in Christ who have the Holy Spirit dwelling in them. I extend the same challenge to young men today who have been programmed to look at girls with lust to instead radically respect them because they have God's Spirit indwelling them. This reality is what will create a healthier sexuality, even for married men and women. It is so easy to follow the world's standards. Radical respect leads us toward sexual integrity. Frankly, it is an easy concept to learn and a difficult concept to follow. Yet it is one of the key lessons of setting sexual standards for our children.

> *You are not your own; you were bought at a price.*
> *Therefore honor God with your body.* (v. 20)

This Scripture lays the foundation for sexual purity. It reminds us that the sacrificial love of Christ brings us life abundant on earth and life eternal. He is the one who demonstrated His love for us by dying for us. He paid the ultimate price. Our response is that we give Him our body. Again the word *body* relates to much more than just our sexuality, but it obviously does include our sexuality. Here is where I believe it is the goal of every parent to help their children commit to sexual purity. It isn't a one-time commitment but rather a continual or constant commitment to self-discipline and living by the Purity Code.

The Purity Code

That last Scripture I quoted (1 Corinthians 6:20) identifies the first area of our child's life that should be committed to God if he or she is to live by the Purity Code: **Honor God with your body.** Not only should we encourage our children to not participate in sexual sin, but they should keep their body healthy in other ways, including eating healthy, exercising, and having good sleep habits. Even good hygiene is a way they can take care of their body, this gift from God.

The second part of the Purity Code is to **renew your mind for the good.** This is based on Romans 12:2: *"Do not conform any longer to the pattern of this world, but be transformed by the renewing of your mind. Then you will be able to test and approve what God's will is—his good, pleasing and perfect will."* No matter what age, a person who lives by the Purity Code needs to tune out the "bad" in culture and tune in the "good." I challenge students to spend even a few minutes a day reading a devotional or Scripture. I challenge them to listen to good music that will lift them up and keep their minds set on positive things. I challenge them to find friends who provide them positive, healthy conversations.

The third part of the Purity Code is to **turn your eyes from worthless things.** I talk to young people about their eyes being a window to their soul. This truth comes straight from Jesus, who said, "The eye is the lamp of the body. If your eyes are good, your whole body will be full of light" (Matthew 6:22). I try to get students to see how our eyes have a deep connection with our mind. Images of everything we see are taken and stored in the brain. And the more negative and sexually explicit stuff we see—whether accidentally or on purpose—the more it will be stuck in our mind.

The final part of the Purity Code is to **guard your heart above all else**. This is based on Proverbs 4:23, which says, "Guard your heart above all else, for it determines the course of your life" (NLT). What a great summary of the lifelong benefits of living by the Purity Code from as young an age as possible.

One of my favorite speaking experiences is challenging students to consider taking a Sexual Purity Pledge. I love the phrase "The Purity Code," which is also the title of the book for preteens in this series. I try to help them see that this isn't just about sexual intercourse, but rather it is a lifelong process of honoring God with their sexuality. When a kid "gets it," I watch the lights go on in his or her head. They realize that by committing to sexual purity, they are, first and foremost, showing honor to God, the Creator of their body, but also that they are fulfilling His desire for His children to be free from carrying one more piece of baggage into an eventual marriage relationship. When Jesus said, "You will know the truth and the truth will set you free," He obviously wasn't just talking about our sexuality. However, a consistent pledge to sexual purity is a road to true freedom for your children and for you. The Purity Code Pledge that follows may be a good first start for you to help lay a strong foundation of sexual integrity with your own child. A printout of the pledge can be made at *www .homeword.com.*

As you help lay the foundation for sexual integrity for kids, a good next step is to give them the practical tools to help set standards that will keep their foundation strong. That's what we will look at in the next chapter.

ENCOURAGING PARENTS, BUILDING FAMILIES

Do you not know that your body is a temple of the Holy Spirit, who is in you, whom you have received from God? You are not your own; you were bought at a price. Therefore honor God with your body.

(1 Corinthians 6:19–20)

The Purity Code Pledge

In honor of God, my family, and my future spouse, I commit my life to sexual purity. **This involves:**

- Honoring God with my **body**.

- Renewing my **mind** for the good.

- Turning my **eyes** from worthless things.

- Guarding my **heart** above all else.

Signature:_____ Date:_____

CHAPTER THREE

Helping Your Kids Set Standards

Rachel was a boy-crazy ninth grader whose cell phone seemed connected to her ear. She really hadn't ever had a boyfriend—at least not a serious relationship—but she fell hard for Ryan. He was a year older. Even her parents thought he was a "hunk." Ryan was a fringe kid in Rachel's youth group. Once, while on a youth group outing, Rachel strayed away with Ryan. They started kissing. The next thing she knew, he was unbuttoning her top. She was petrified, but he kept going, and she froze from stopping him. That night Rachel and Ryan did everything but have sexual intercourse.

Before that night, Rachel certainly had thought about sex from time to time, but she had never thought about setting standards or limits; she didn't think she would ever be in a compromising situation. Her parents hadn't talked to her much about relationships. They were busy with work, home, church, and basically trying to get through each day intact. Her father teased her about boys and her mother told her to be careful because "all boys have only one thing on their minds." That was about the extent of the information she got on relationships from her parents. They definitely had never talked with her about how far was too far. Her youth worker had done some teaching on sexuality but never specifically on setting standards. Now, after the experience with Ryan, she didn't know quite how to feel about it. They hadn't gone all the way, and she did like most of the feelings, yet she felt some shame for what had occurred. She told her girl friend she didn't want to do what she had done with Ryan again, but the very next week it happened again.

Rachel's story is the story of millions of young people today. Most of the time their parents have not talked to them about setting standards, and often, kids end up going further than they wish they had gone. There are at least three reasons:

Reason #1. Pressure to Conform

Peer pressure is very powerful. If a young person's friends are experimenting with promiscuous behavior or pornography on the Internet, the odds are great that without parental input, he or she will too. Kids imitate their friends.

Reason #2. Emotional Involvement That Exceeds Their Maturity Level

This is a major reason kids make unwise sexual decisions. Let's pick on Rachel for a moment. She is fourteen and has a poor self-image. "Prince Charming" comes into her life. She is "in love." Her parents tell her it's "puppy love," but the fact remains that puppy love is real to puppies! She is emotionally involved with Ryan and yet, because of her age, low maturity level, and lack of standards, she gives in and regrets it later.

Reason #3. Lack of Value-Centered Sex Education From Home

I know this sounds like a broken record, but kids will make healthier decisions when they have healthy parental involvement with sex education.

When you think about establishing sexual standards, it's natural to think first about issues such as kissing and how far is too far. These are important subjects to discuss, but I believe standards must also be set regarding clothing choices and modesty in general, media usage, dealing with visual temptations, and even alcohol and drug use. These are topics that can be discussed with younger and older children alike.

The question is, How do we as parents help our kids set standards without sounding like a nag or being the morality police at all times? It is a good question with no simple answers. I hope it helps to realize that parents shouldn't be running a popularity contest with their preteens and teens. As I said earlier, our job is to raise responsible young adults, not simply to make them happy at all costs. If your kids like you all of the time, you probably have a parenting flaw in your life.

The best way to help your children set healthy standards is to face the issues and try to keep the conversation positive. Talk often and be blunt when you need to, depending on the age of your kids. Sometimes parents don't want to bring up certain issues because they think their kids are too innocent or not ready for some other reason. Just let me urge you not to wait too long. Remember that the latest facts tell us that 65 percent of non-virgins say their parents think they are still virgins.[1]

Setting God-Honoring Standards

Modesty

Modesty sounds like such an old-fashioned word. It conjures up thoughts of legalistic calls for ankle-length dresses and turtlenecks. Modesty is actually much more than wearing non-revealing clothes. Modesty applies to the way we act, dress, and live.

A number of years ago I was a youth worker in a local church. My wife and I took twelve students on a houseboat trip along the California River Delta. It was an odd mix of students. We had eight beautiful upperclassman girls and three younger guys. After a few days, the girls began to get very comfortable in their environment. They were treating the boys like little brothers. I noticed that the clothes were getting skimpier and skimpier. The girls were into tanning, so they would undo the back straps of their swimsuits and ask their "little brothers" to put suntan lotion on their backs. When bedtime approached, their outfits of choice were a long T-shirt (obviously bra-less) and underpants. I knew these girls well, but I was very surprised at their behavior. Needless to say, the three younger boys on the trip were having the time of their lives. Their focus wasn't on the Bible studies, but rather those beautiful bodies parading around the houseboat.

My wife and I finally called a girls-only meeting one evening after they were ready for bed. All the girls but one arrived in a T-shirt and basically nothing more. In their minds, it was safe to dress like that because they were with only three younger boys and a safe, married youth worker and his wife. One young woman sat next to Cathy, and I actually handed her a pillow to cover up what she was showing everyone. Nervously I said, "It's time for a talk about modesty from a guy!" I told them they were all beautiful young women, and it was important for them to hear from a guy what goes on in a guy's mind when he sees skin or shapes that are barely covered. If I remember right, I said, "Guys are visual. When you dress immodestly, you cause males to lust at you. It's been said that showing off more than you are willing to give is false advertising! There are two types of girls who wear revealing clothes. One knows exactly what she is doing, and the other (and I put most of these girls in this category) has little idea how she is making guys look at her."

I wish I could say that each of the girls immediately agreed with me. Basically, many were defensive and somewhat emotional. Still, I held my ground.

I believe it is both Mom's and Dad's responsibility to teach about modesty and the effects of immodesty. As a father of girls, I think it is just as important for dads to discuss it with their daughters as it is for moms to speak with their sons. I remember a time when one of my daughters was sixteen and she bought a swimsuit that I thought was too revealing with her own money. She couldn't take the suit back, so I bought it from her and went with her to buy another one, which cost me even more money. That was a tough financial decision for this Scotch Irish male, but now that I look back, the lesson was worth the expense.

Whenever possible, avoid taking on the role of Fashion Police. Many parents need to keep quiet about the latest fashion statement so that they can be heard on the more-important modesty issue. I realize this is a bigger issue for girls than guys, but it does come up with young men as well.

Finally, depending on the situation, you might want to challenge your child with this thought, passed along by Hayley DiMarco, who is one of my favorite authors on this subject. In her book *Sexy Girls*, she quotes a youth pastor who said, "If you're showing skin regularly, ask yourself, 'Who are my fashion role models?' and, 'Are they living a worthy and holy life?'"[2]

Garbage In/Garbage Out: How Media Changes the Standards

Media is another area where standards are important for teaching healthy sexuality. Like you, I'm guessing, I wish the media was not so "in our face" with amoral or immoral sexuality. Unfortunately, this is not the case, and as optimistic as I am about life, it's not going to get better. If anything, the negative media influences will continue to slide downward.

The standard I teach my children is the "Garbage In/Garbage Out" principle. You might know it already: If you make poor decisions about what enters your mind, negative things will come out; if you put good things into your mind, then good things will come out.

Parents are in the protection business, and we have to walk the fine line of keeping unhealthy images away from our children while teaching them how to have the self-control to deal with what bombards their eyes and minds every day.

Media is not neutral. It is not either all bad or all good, but it certainly is powerful. Just consider the recent studies that tell us that the average young person can see fourteen thousand acts of intercourse or sexual innuendos on primetime TV each year. They will also spend more time on the Internet than watching TV in a week, and a majority of kids will accidentally or not-so-accidentally view pornography each month. This just can't be good for the mind. Much of the music on the top stations has blatant sexual references. There is simply a battle for our children's minds, and we have to help our children set standards and limits or they will be in for a life of struggle.

As I stated previously, your job is to become a student of your child's culture. You will need to listen to what they listen to, watch what they watch, and read what they read. As you become an "expert," though, be careful to not come off as a parent who reacts negatively to everything they do. It is a much more effective, though frankly difficult, task to teach and train your kids to set their own healthy standards with media.

Frequently, we parents have to first examine our own behavior and standards. If Mom and Dad watch raunchy movies, expect their children to do the same. Children see, children do. As you evaluate your child's media choices, enter into dialogue, not monologue. When my children got older, I allowed them to watch the MTV Video Music Awards as long as I was watching the show with them and able to go out for frozen yogurt afterward and discuss the pros and the (many) cons from the experience.

In order to help kids set standards with media and keep the garbage from influencing them, I suggest you create agreements regarding music, TV programs, movies, and the Internet. Spell it out as clearly as possible. (Sample agreements are provided in chapter 5.) Whenever possible, allow your kids to help set the standards. Kids support what they help create. Together, come up with a reasonable agreement of what music, movies, TV shows, and Internet influences can and cannot be allowed in your home. Talk ahead about the amount of hours your kids can watch TV or play video games. In many ways, you are creating a contract with your kids that can help them monitor their media influence.

The Garbage In/Garbage Out principle is a great code to learn while young. Paul explained this concept best when he wrote, "Whatever is true, whatever is pure, whatever is lovely, whatever is admirable—if anything is excellent or praise-worthy—think about such things. Whatever you have learned or received or heard from me, or seen in me—put it into practice. And the God of peace will be with you" (Philippians 4: 8–9).

Ultimately, our job is to train our children to put good and right things in their minds. This doesn't just happen. We must proactively help them. We do it by modeling right behavior, providing lots of healthy alternatives, and teaching our children how media can influence their moldable minds.

How Far Is Too Far?

Most youth workers would agree that even kids from the strongest of homes will eventually wonder, *How far is too far?* As you read in chapter 2, the Bible has clear wisdom about sexuality. Even so, there have been many times I wish Scripture contained more specific words. Within the Christian world there are several opinions about physical affection before marriage. Some say that a man and woman shouldn't even kiss until their wedding day. Others have different definitions of healthy, God-honoring boundaries.

The one principle I would remind you to keep at the forefront of your mind is that when it comes to standards, help your child set limits before he or she ever gets to "Inspiration Point." Also consider your child's age and maturity level. Some people will disagree with me, but I believe it is important at the right age to talk about and demystify certain physical components of a potential sexual relationship.

The next chapter presents more detail about how and when to talk with kids about sex and sexuality. For now, though, here's a list of topics that I think would be helpful to cover. Find times to be very frank about the potential dangers, pitfalls, and experiences that go along with each of these physical components.

- Holding hands casually
- Holding hands constantly
- Hugging
- Light kissing
- Strong, passionate kissing
- French kissing
- Fondling of the breast
- Fondling of the sexual organs
- Oral sex
- Mutual masturbation
- Sexual intercourse[3]

I think it is very appropriate and necessary to also talk about back rubs and massages, tickling and teasing, as well as napping together. One mother I know admitted to me that when she was in high school, all she wanted to do was be close with her boyfriend, so she saw nothing wrong with back rubs, tickling, and napping together. However, within a fairly short time, the young man couldn't handle his hormones, and she found herself compromising her values and boundaries. She told me that she wished her parents would have talked to her about such subjects.

Self-Control

Too often parents put all their energy and time into dealing with homework hassles, hauling kids around town, and other things that are important, but none of them is as important as helping their kids build character into their lives. The character issue of self-control and self-discipline is huge when it comes to setting healthy sexual standards. You can do all the teaching you want, but almost every kid will at times experience temptations and need to develop the self-control to live by healthy standards. For most children, this just doesn't come naturally; that's why we need to teach them practical ways to discern sensual images and stay free of pornography, as well as the importance of accountability.

In their book *Every Man's Battle*, Fred Stoeker and Steve Arterburn coin a great phrase for a technique that all of us (men and women, boys and girls) can use to minimize visual temptations and live by healthy standards. It's called "bouncing the eyes."[4] When we or our children see a sensual image—whether a beauty in a skimpy swimsuit, sexy women and men in an advertisement, someone jogging by, you name it—it's important to bounce our eyes. As quickly as possible, discipline yourself to turn your eyes off the image. This principle helps kids realize that it's natural to notice sexual images, but we shouldn't stare. That's when the mind takes over and lust can develop. Boys have more of a problem with this than girls, but the number of young women sharing stories of lust and poor habits with sensual images is ever increasing.

Another troubling increase is occurring in the number of young people in general who are viewing pornography online and elsewhere. This development is, in my opinion, one of the scariest issues of the new sexual revolution. Sure, kids have always looked at porn, but it just wasn't as easily accessible as it is now.

Teach your kids to have zero tolerance for porn. Stoeker and Arterburn call this "starving the eyes."[5] Kids must literally make a commitment to cut off any access to pornographic images. One of the many problems of viewing pornography is that your mind takes a picture of the image. And sadly, millions of young people today have very inappropriate images stored in their minds. Pornography is extremely addicting, and for many, it can escalate.

The Porn Addiction Progression

1. Viewing pornography

2. Addiction

3. Escalation

4. Desensitization

5. Acting Out Sexually

In today's world, kids cannot help but see very unhealthy sexual images. As parents, you can help kids by teaching them the negative consequences of viewing pornography (see the next chapter), as well as setting boundaries related to computer use. For one thing, there should not be a computer with Internet access in a child's bedroom. The temptations are just too strong.

Because the world does bring kids so many temptations today, it is important to teach them the significance of accountability. As a young person reaches middle school, it is very possible for them to find an accountability partner or group to help them work through the temptations of life. I know a young woman who hosts a group of middle school girls every Wednesday after school to talk with them, and they all have each other to hold themselves accountable to the higher standards they have set for themselves in many areas of their lives. Although most adults don't have accountability relationships, they would be much better off if they shared their standards of behavior with trusted accountability partners. How much better it is to help kids set a standard of accountability early in their lives.

Sex and Alcohol

Parents will often teach their children not to drink and drive. Obviously, driving while under the influence, the number-one killer of young people, should be discussed. But more and more we are realizing that driving is not the only thing kids are doing under the influence. Kids who drink alcohol also tend to be involved in much more at-risk behaviors than if they don't drink. As many as 70 percent of college students admit to having engaged in sexual activity primarily as a result of being under the influence of alcohol, or to having sex they wouldn't have had if they had been sober.[6] Other studies have found that sexually active teens are far more likely than celibate peers to be involved in a variety of destructive behaviors, including drug and alcohol use, school delinquency, and attempted suicide.

Researchers from Indiana University-Bloomington and Indiana University Medical School surveyed over fifteen hundred twelve- to sixteen-year-olds about their lifestyles. Their study, published in the journal *Pediatrics*, found that 63 percent of boys and 36 percent of girls said they'd had intercourse at least once. Sexually experienced girls were five times more likely than virgins to have been suspended from school and more likely to have tried suicide. Boys with sexual experience were six times more likely to have used alcohol and five times more likely to have used marijuana. Obviously, all these problems are interrelated, but they often do come back to drug and alcohol use.

As parents, we must be very intentional about drug-proofing our children. If we are going to help kids set standards about their sexual lives, we also have to help them set standards for drug and alcohol use. The two issues really go together. Steve Arterburn and I created a Drug-Proof Plan in our book *How to Talk to Your Kids About Drugs.*[7] The Drug-Proof Plan involves the following areas:

Education: Parents must obtain the knowledge they need about drugs, alcohol, and addiction. The information must then be passed along to their kids. Unfortunately, this part of the plan is often neglected because parents sometimes assume their children already have the right information. Parents who gamble on others doing the educating are asking for trouble.

Prevention: Prevention involves rewards for responsible behavior and restrictions following irresponsible behavior. This is a part of a good overall parenting strategy that encourages kids to make right decisions and lets them immediately feel the consequences for poor choices.

Identification: When parents become aware that their children are using drugs or alcohol, the problem must be immediately evaluated. "Secret behavior" should not be allowed. Kids who are experimenting are often sneaky about their life. In this part of the plan, kids are not left to confront the problem on their own or work out how to get out of it by themselves. It is a family problem.

Intervention: If the problem develops and is identified, this part of the plan allows for fast, appropriate parental action to extinguish the undesirable behavior.

Treatment: Professional treatment comes in many forms, but if it is needed, nothing else can be substituted for it. An important part of the plan is knowing what treatment resources are available and how to use them.

Supportive Follow-Up: This could also be called "relapse prevention." It enables the family to be part of the ongoing recovery process rather than to unknowingly destroy the foundations of a lifetime of sobriety.

Self-Evaluation: Parents can't intervene effectively in the lives of their children unless the adults have made some positive decisions about their own involvement with alcohol and drugs.

The Bottom Line

The bottom line is that preparing our kids to be responsible adults is not always an easy job, but the parents who have the best results are those who help their children set standards before situations and choices arise. These same parents offer a lot of grace and are intentional about helping their kids make wise decisions. They also live by the same healthy standards as their kids. Finally, they find ways to talk about healthy sexuality, which is what we will look at in the next chapter.

CHAPTER FOUR

How and When to Talk With Your Kids About Sex and Sexuality

The day had arrived! Little seven-year-old Jeremy had come home from school, sat at the kitchen table, and blurted out the big question, "Hey, Mom, what is sex?" Jeremy's mother tried to stay calm. She and Jeremy's dad had anticipated the when and even hows of *the* sex conversation, but it wasn't supposed to happen at seven years old, and it wasn't supposed to take place when her husband was away on a business trip. Even so, in somewhat of a panic, she decided that this was the time to have "the talk." After all, Jeremy was curious, and she should be ready with an answer. She placed a large plate of cookies and a tall glass of milk in front of him and took a deep breath before launching into her sex education lesson.

Jeremy sat quietly listening, eating all the cookies and drinking the milk. Sometimes his eyes were as big as saucers as his mom described in great detail the important aspects of human sexuality. In forty-five minutes she covered the male and female reproductive systems, relationships, where babies come from, and even some personal information about her honeymoon with his dad. She drew diagrams of sperm and eggs and gave him all the gory details, wishing all along that she had the help of her husband. Finally she was finished with this most intriguing lecture.

"Jeremy, do you have any questions?"

Her son, who had been silent but attentive the whole time, fumbled in his back pocket and pulled out a crumpled piece of paper. After staring at it for a minute, he asked, "This is my soccer application, and I'm still not sure what to put on it where it says, 'Sex: M or F'?"

Yes, as Jeremy's mom discovered, discussing the "S" word can induce panic in even the most confident parent. Just what do you share, and when . . . and how?

Some parents talk to their child about sex and sexuality too early, and others wait too long. They rely solely upon circumstances and chance to make it happen. However, it really is better when we have a guide and a thought-out purpose. It is also important to keep in mind *age-appropriate developmental issues.*

For Cathy and me this didn't come easy. Our parents didn't talk to us about sex and sexuality—although I do remember something my father said before leaving me with my grandma while he and my mom took a trip to Florida. "Jim," he said, "I don't want you and your girlfriend to get physically involved while we're gone because you have some important basketball games this week, and being with your girlfriend in *that* way could affect your ability to play well." He then turned and left the room, leaving me at age sixteen to figure out what in the world he was even talking about!

Years later, when Cathy and I became parents, we had basically no clue about teaching healthy sexuality to our own kids. When our first daughter, Christy, was about one, I vaguely remember helping her learn the names of body parts. We focused on the nose, ears, eyes, hands, feet, etc., but missed some pretty important private parts. By the time our next child, Rebecca, came along, we corrected the situation and taught her the proper terms for those private body parts. And then at the most inopportune moments, like in a crowded store or in the middle of a church service, she would shout that a particular body part itched! People would look at us like we had corrupted our child. To say the least, our sex-education "method" was trial-and-error at first.

Creating a Plan and a Purpose

Cathy and I knew we had to look to the wisdom of others who had gone before us. The Bible says, "Without wise leadership, a nation falls; there is safety in having many advisors" (Proverbs 11:14 NLT). We sought the advice of parents who had already helped their children develop healthy attitudes about their sexuality, and we also devoured excellent books on the subject. From our reading and inquiry, we learned that experts have identified certain age groupings when children normally experience significant developmental changes—mentally, physically, and even spiritually. We decided to divide up the teaching and training into age-appropriate stages: ages three to five, six to nine, ten to thirteen, and fourteen to eighteen. These age groupings weren't hard and firm, but they have been a good guide.

Cathy and I made a list of the topics we felt we needed to cover, and we basically began to place them in the appropriate developmental category.[1] Then, about every six months, we would take a half day and reevaluate what we felt needed to be discussed with our kids. We did this in the areas of sexuality, faith, educational issues, character traits, and other relevant topics.

Building the Foundation

Of course, teaching children about healthy sexuality is much more than passing along information. It is about encouraging wholesome relationships and attitudes. It is about laying a foundation for a lifelong, healthy "theology of sexuality" (as introduced in chapter 2).

We parents want our children to know that God created sexuality, and in the light of marriage, He sees it as very good. We want our children to know that God wants the best for each of them in this area of their lives. He is not the great killjoy but rather the creator and sustainer of life. We want our children to have healthy God-honoring attitudes and behaviors when it comes to human sexuality.

The popular culture of the day often teaches through words and innuendos that sex is dirty and selfish, so at appropriate age levels we must teach our kids how to respond to the negative images and messages they see in the culture. As parents, we are to provide positive role models for our children as we introduce these important topics to our children.

Too many parents think all that needs to happen is that they have the "birds and bees" talk *once,* when a child is about thirteen. Nothing could be further from the best way to deal with this issue. We should start the conversations when our children are very young and continue them through young adulthood. The more ordinary and ongoing the conversations, the easier it will be for you as a parent and for your children to have healthy attitudes about sex and relationships.

Age-Appropriate Topics

This section contains general concepts and topics I suggest introducing and discussing with your child at certain age-appropriate levels. As you do, be intentional and purposeful in *what* you want to teach, but hold loosely to *how* and *when* you teach things. Just recently, I sat with my daughter over frozen yogurt and tried to offer a lecture on a particular issue. It didn't go over half as well as if I had waited for an appropriate discussion time that felt more natural. For younger children, also know that it's more than okay to briefly introduce a topic at one stage and come back to it on a deeper or more explicit level at the next stage.

The most effective way to teach healthy sexuality is to take advantage of spontaneous teachable moments whenever possible instead of more formal talks. Use everyday situations and life experiences to get your message across. Personally, some of my best conversations with my children over the years have been prompted by a TV show, a song on the radio, a problem one of the kids' friends was having, a story in the news, and the list goes on. You might also want to encourage some teachable moments by sharing books with your child, like *The Purity Code*, which is written for preteens and young teens, as well as *Accept Nothing Less* and the other resources in the PURE FOUNDATIONS series that we have developed at HomeWord.

God Made Boys and God Made Girls (ages 3 to 5)

The overriding theme for this age level is providing a basic foundation that God created you and your body. He created boys and girls and moms and dads. He created each body part. He loves us and wants us to honor Him with our body. We even need to be introducing the differences between males and females to three- to five-year-olds. We also need to bring up personal safety issues and what is proper and inappropriate touch from a stranger, a baby-sitter, or even a family member.

The discussions should be comfortable and occur often. Questions can be answered to the degree of their understanding. You want your kids to feel good about their bodies and comfortable talking with you about any of the issues they bring up.

A Time of Curiosity (ages 6 to 9)

This is a developmental stage when kids are very curious. At this stage you begin to introduce basic sexuality. On a light level you will want to answer the question, "Where do babies come from?" God created males and females differently and with a purpose. With the key element of their curiosity in mind, we need to introduce very basic human anatomy and how God is a part of each family from conception through death.

Keeping Yourself Pure (ages 10 to 13)—The Purity Code

One of the important messages in this developmental stage is the fact that our bodies are gifts from God and that we can commit to the Purity Code. A lot of change is taking place at this stage, and puberty is the time when these changes are much more apparent. This is a key stage to introduce that sexuality is a gift from God and is to be used in obedience to Him. By the end of this stage, most everything should be addressed—from guy/girl relationships to pornography on the Internet, cultural influences, peer pressure, modesty, and flirting, as well as grace and forgiveness.

God's Best for Your Body, Mind, and Heart (ages 14 to 18)

During this stage your job is not done. Conversations and parental instruction need to take place on dating, setting standards, sexual abuse, how far is too far, learning to radically respect members of the opposite sex, drugs, alcohol and sex, partying, and sexual integrity decisions. (These topics and more are included in my upcoming book *Accept Nothing Less*, which is written for this age group.) By this stage, no conversation should be off limits with parents. Kids are vulnerable. They are going through an experimental stage in life where sometimes they disown previously held values while trying new behaviors. Blunt, unashamedly moral conversations with your kids about anything and everything make it easier for your kids to navigate their sexuality at this important stage. They might need to be reminded that God is still present in their sexuality like He is in other areas of their lives. If parents lecture or nag, they will close their child's spirit to discussion, but if they can be open and show real care and concern, their children will continue to be open to discussion.

Rites of Passage

Not to be overlooked in this discussion of age-appropriate teaching is the wonderful fact that our children's bodies are growing and changing. Milestones in life, like moving from one developmental stage to the next, should be celebrated. Cathy and I created two rites-of-passage experiences for our children that I highly recommend. One involves blessing a child's physical maturation at puberty, and the other relates more to dating and sexual purity.

Rites-of-passage experiences, whether formal or informal, are markers for your kids to remember a time when you recognized and blessed their development.[2] I have really found them to be wonderful ways for parents to connect with their children. When teaching healthy sexuality—or any other topic, for that matter—*relationship* is the key word. Kids crave relationship with their parents. This might be easier to see now when your child is young, but it continues to be true as kids grow older. As you communicate your love and care for your kids, you bless them with a strong sense of security and value. You are given only so many times to connect with your kids, so please don't miss it.

Puberty

When each of our girls first hit puberty, Cathy took them for a mother-daughter overnight stay at a nice hotel. If we would have had boys, it would have been me (though I would have taken them on a campout with fishing or surfing, and no showering!). My wife and daughter would have a fun meal and then go shopping for a new outfit. (Their language of love!) Then Cathy would read a book with the girls much like *The Purity Code* and talk about issues related to puberty. It basically became a very open conversation about sexuality and sexual intercourse. She tried to make the conversation a dialogue and, depending on the child, it worked okay, but not perfectly. Still, important information was passed on, and the rite of passage was a catalyst for many other conversations about healthy sexuality.

Let me mention that I don't think the more informative and serious talks about our sexuality always have to be men with boys and women with girls, but it seems to sometimes be easier. Many single parents do an excellent job talking about puberty, and they obviously don't have the luxury of same-sex discussions. Regardless of who takes the lead in the discussions, it is more important to have the dialogue than which parent actually does it.

Whether you provide a similar rite-of-passage experience for your child, or he or she is simply in that ten-and-a-half to thirteen-year-old age range, it is important to discuss the details of puberty. Kids begin to see and feel changes going on inside and outside of their bodies, but many don't get the perspective of their parents. Talk to your child before and while these changes are taking place. I also recommend that together you go through a book or booklet with anatomy diagrams and all.[3] Make sure you don't forget to discuss topics and facts that are often uncomfortable to talk about, because if you don't discuss them, who will do it in a way you would be happy with?

Talking About Our Bodies

Males

- Penis
- Foreskin
- Scrotum
- Seminal vesicles
- Prostate
- Testicles
- Sperm
- Erections
- Ejaculation

Females

- Ovaries
- Fallopian tubes
- Uterus
- Cervix
- Vagina and vaginal canal
- Hymen
- Urethra
- Labia
- Clitoris
- Vulva
- Eggs
- Menstruation

General

- Sexual intercourse
- Wet dreams
- Pregnancy and birth

A Commitment to Purity

The second rite-of-passage for our girls (this time with me) came when each one turned sixteen. This special time was centered on making a commitment to the Purity Code, and was more relational than informational.

Cathy and I decided that each girl's first "date" would be an overnight getaway with Dad. We went to the city of their choice within a two-hour drive. Christy chose San Diego, Becca chose Palm Springs, and Heidi chose Beverly Hills. (Try finding a cheap hotel in Beverly Hills!) I took them to a nice dinner, repeated the shopping routine from their first rite of passage, and generally had a lot of fun. The serious side to the overnight was when I presented my daughter with some relevant Scripture and a challenge toward sexual purity. I mostly used the Scripture quoted in this book's chapter 2. Then, each girl received a purity ring as a reminder of God's commitment to them and their commitment to sexual integrity and purity.

When it comes to helping your children remain sexually pure, don't underestimate offering your own affection toward them. In a UCLA study, it was found that the average person needs eight to ten meaningful touches for them to thrive. I am convinced that there are thousands of sexually promiscuous kids who were looking for wholesome affection, but it turned inappropriate from someone other than their parents. If you grew up in a family that didn't show appropriate affection and now you don't see its importance or somehow it feels awkward, here are three words to consider as you think about showering your children with affection: Get over it! Despite your background, find the strength to bring appropriate affection to your kids from childhood through young adulthood and beyond.

I know the next list will look a bit daunting, but the topics below are the kinds of topics I believe parents must be talking with their kids about at an appropriate age. These topics are covered in my books for preteens and teens, *The Purity Code* and *Accept Nothing Less*. I find it best when you and your spouse can choose topics for a six-month period of time and then look for ways to bring up the subject. It's called "planned spontaneity." You can look for opportunities from conversation with your kids, television programs, magazines, music, or anything that you think might be an opening for good discussion.

The Topic List

- Appropriate touch and inappropriate touch
- Correct names of body parts
- Puberty and changes
- Physical difference between males and females
- Cultural influences and learning to discern right from wrong
- Radical respect for the opposite sex
- Your body is the temple of God
- Pornography
- Internet influence
- Sexual abuse
- Lust
- Sexual purity pledge
- The power of friendships
- Movie, music, and other media influences
- Grace and forgiveness
- Emotions

- Self-image
- Peer pressure
- Building a theology of healthy sexuality
- Flirting
- Partying
- True beauty
- Clothes and modesty issues
- Your mind is a sex organ too
- How far is too far?
- Sexually transmitted diseases (STDs)
- AIDS
- Dating
- Technical virginity (today's culture's description of doing everything but intercourse)
- Oral sex
- Cohabitation
- Secondary virginity
- Hooking up/friends with benefits
- Abusive relationships
- Compromising your values
- Consequences of poor choices and sexual behavior
- Drug and alcohol use and abuse
- Christians dating non-Christians

- Depression and sex
- Crisis issues (suicide, cutting, eating disorders, the death of a friend, abuse, etc.)
- Nutrition
- Hygiene
- Reproduction
- Sexual intercourse
- Eating disorders
- Date rape
- Birth control
- Getting along with parents
- Gender identity confusion and homosexuality (See chapter 8 for advice about talking with your child about this topic.)
- Masturbation
- Setting boundaries
- Self-control and self-discipline
- Accountability
- Temptation
- Unwed pregnancies
- Abortion
- Why wait?
- Unconditional love

This is not an exhaustive list, but these topics may cause you to come up with others or more details on certain subjects.

As we deal with the how, when, and where of discussing sexual issues with our children, remember that every child is different, even those in the same age grouping. Parents need to have a sense of humor about the whole thing. Sometimes we get it right and sometimes, as the following story shows, we get it a bit wrong.

Little Tony was staying with his grandmother for a few days. He'd been playing outside with neighbor friends when he came into the house and asked, "Grandma, what is that called when two people are sleeping in the same room and one is on top of the other?"

Grandma was taken aback, but she decided to tell him the truth. "It's called sexual intercourse, darling."

Little Tony replied with a quick "oh, okay," and went back outside to play. A few minutes later he returned and declared forcefully, "Grandma, it is not called sexual intercourse. It's called bunk beds! And Jimmy's mom wants to talk to you!"

The next chapter isn't an easy one. We will look at the physical and emotional consequences of sexual promiscuity. It's the kind of information we must share with our children at an age-appropriate time to help them make wise decisions that will last a lifetime.

CHAPTER FIVE

Sex Outside of Marriage: Choices and Consequences

I firmly believe that young people today have the will and the ability to remain sexually abstinent, but much depends on what role their parents take. This doesn't mean that teaching healthy sexuality is easy or that victory happens with every child. Rather, the statistics point in another direction, in large part, because so many parents have been absolutely silent in their children's sex education. People are even fighting abstinence education in our schools, saying abstinence education will move our country "backward" in reducing teen pregnancy. How exactly abstinence will result in more teen pregnancies is still unclear and, frankly, laughable.

Abstinence works. There are no losers with sexual abstinence. Studies show that abstinence education is the most effective way to keep kids from getting pregnant, contracting sexually transmitted diseases, and having to live with the emotional and spiritual consequences connected with the "instant intimacy" of early sexual encounters.

It's a big goal to help your kids practice sexual integrity, but again, it is achievable and it is worth the time and effort. Just ask the people who have chosen to wait until marriage, as well as those who have suffered the consequences of unwise decisions. Both groups would give their strong support for the biblical view of sexual abstinence before marriage. There is such a thing as safe and beautiful sex, and it happens when people have waited for this God-given experience until after the wedding. As parents, it is part of our job description to lovingly make sure our children understand the negative consequences of unwise choices.

The Hazards of Early Sexualization and Sexual Promiscuity

Fifteen-year-old Julie Thomas (not her real name) came from a very strong and committed Christian home. She attended a Christian school until the eighth grade, and her parents were active in their church and leaders in the world of Christian ministry. When Julie developed some pain and itching in her genital area, her mother took her for her first visit to a gynecologist. The diagnosis: herpes. It soon came out that Julie had gone to a dance with a boy who talked her into doing everything but sexual intercourse. Julie had no idea that what she was doing was risky. Today, Julie would say she made a very poor decision that one night with a boy who meant nothing to her.

Stories like Julie's are why parents so often try to scare their kids into "not doing it." After all, teenagers are known for their it-won't-happen-to-me beliefs. Interestingly, new studies on brain development have shown that the part of the brain that keeps people from making rash decisions is not fully developed until *after* the teen years. This is all the more reason why kids are vulnerable to a number of issues that make sex outside of marriage very risky.

Without trying to make this chapter too negative, let's tackle three of the biggest obstacles your kids will face in the coming years.

Media

Studies show that kids with early exposure to sexually explicit media in TV programs, movies, magazines, music, and on the Internet were much more likely to have had sexual intercourse when re-interviewed two years later than their peers who had a lighter sexual media diet. A study reported in the *Pediatrics* medical journal in 2006 showed that exposure to sexual content between ages twelve to fourteen increased the likelihood of early sex among teenagers by 30 percent, even after taking into account other factors known to reduce the likelihood of teen sex, such as parental disapproval and getting good grades. This study and hundreds of others show us that early sexualization in the lives of our children puts them at much greater risk. Kids sense it too. A national survey reports that three out of four fifteen- to seventeen-year-olds believe that sexual content on TV, including music videos, influences the sexual behavior of their peers.

As I mentioned in a previous chapter, we can't keep our children in a bubble. That would be damaging, but it doesn't mean there shouldn't be limits. Media viewing in the home must be monitored. Media-viewing contracts like the one that follows can be helpful.

Frankly, you aren't running a popularity contest as a parent. You are, in fact, in the protection business. Sexually explicit material will only increase as the years go by, so parents' jobs are even more difficult because we must give our children the tools to make good and wise decisions themselves.

I mentioned to a group of friends that the average high-schooler watches MTV ten hours a week. Most of those friends hadn't ever monitored what their kids were viewing on the music channel. I encouraged them to watch a few hours. The next week they came back and reported being shocked at what they saw. When MTV was just starting out, its president and CEO at the time, Robert Pittman, said in an interview with *Parents of Teenagers* magazine, "Early on, we made a key decision that we would be the voice of young America. We were building more than just a channel; we were building a culture."[2] Today, not only does MTV play music videos and somewhat raunchy reality shows, it also helps dictate fashion and dance trends. "Our goal," Pittman said, "is to make MTV the leading authority on young-adult culture worldwide." Pittman was prophetic with those words over twenty-five years ago.

Media-Viewing Contract

Music Agreement:

Music may be played in the home _____ hours per day/week. _____ are the only acceptable styles of music to be listened to anywhere (home, car, school, friend's house, etc.).

TV/Movie-Viewing Agreement:

The TV may be on in the home _____ hours per day/week. Television programs with a rating of _____ are not acceptable in our home. _____ are not acceptable TV programs in our home. The movie ratings that are acceptable for viewing are _____. The family agreement about MTV (or any other music television channel) is _____. TV shows that are appropriate to watch together as a family are _____. Movies that support the biblical standards of our family are_____.

Internet Usage Agreement:

The amount of time each individual will spend online will be no more than _____ hours per day. Web-surfing will be limited to educational, Christian, or other family-friendly sites only. Unsolicited e-mail and forwards with attachments will be deleted unopened. Internet filters will be used at all times.[1]

In our family, social networking sites such as MySpace and Facebook will/will not be used. If allowed, as the parent, I will have total access to the site as one of your "friends." The family decision on gaming is _____ (list types of games, length of playing time, etc.).

Signature:_____ Date:_____

Unfortunately, too many of the teen and preteen heroes today are not very good role models for this generation. I used to feel a bit of anger at these young idols with such troubling morals. Now, along with many others, I feel deeply sorry for them and I am pained by their emptiness. The problem is that they are still role models. Even Madonna, the most popular female vocalist for over two decades, had this to say about her peers: "The actors and singers and entertainers I know are emotional cripples. Really healthy people aren't in this business, let's face it." Madonna said this years before Britney Spears, Lindsay Lohan, and Paris Hilton were even teenagers, but her voice was also prophetic. All this to say, media influences our children for good and bad, and exposure to sexually explicit and immoral behavior does cause harm to our children.

Pornography

Perhaps pornography, more than any other issue of today's culture, has the greatest chance of bringing down the morals and values of this generation. Studies tell us that the greatest new users of pornography are twelve- to seventeen-year-old boys. The girls, however, are catching up. All the while, the multi-billion-dollar pornography industry is reaching into the souls of this generation and wreaking havoc. It is so powerful that it can snatch any kid in any house today.

A thirteen-year-old boy at our church was looking for a new baseball glove online. A large sporting-goods chain in our area is called Chicks Sporting Goods. We all call it "Chicks" for short. He innocently typed the word "Chicks" into a search engine, thinking that he was going to find the store's new baseball glove selection. What he found were pornography sites, and lots of them. His first exposure to porn took him on a journey that caused him to daily, sometimes for hours at a time, look at awful porn. This was a good kid, from a strong family, with high morals, and he just got caught in the maze of porn addiction. When the family finally found out (they began to suspect something when he was on the computer in the middle of the night and his grades were dropping), they did the right thing and got their son help. However, that young boy will have thousands of vivid images stored in his brain and subconscious.

Information on the effects of porn is very prevalent today. I don't need to add much more on the subject, especially when you can find great resources if you are looking for this kind of information.[3] Needless to say, pornography is fantasy. Fantasy and pornography are closely related links to sexual addiction. Pornography is a tool for going beyond reality, and, once used, it is difficult to live without. That's why parents must have zero tolerance for porn in the home. Monitor your computers, talk to your kids about 1-900 pay-per-call sex lines (because of Web availability on cell phones, pornography is now accessible anytime, anywhere), magazines, music groups, and music videos. Help them understand that when porn is used, they can easily become a sex addict. In fact, sexual addiction among young people is growing, and for many, it becomes a strong obsessive compulsion similar to the intensity of alcohol, drug, and gambling addictions. Sexual addiction breaks families apart, causes people to view the opposite sex as objects, and tears at the very moral fiber of really good people. A parent can:

- Speak to their kids about all the ways porn can enter their life
- Monitor computers
- Fill out a form at the post office to not receive sexually explicit material
- Review all music, DVDs, video games, and magazines coming into your home
- Encourage healthy sex education at home and in your churches
- Speak with other parents about your concerns
- Speak to your school PTA about sponsoring programs

The days are over when pornography was confined to a dark section of town at XXX-rated movie theatres. Pornography is distributed through what was once safe channels, like cable TV, bookstores, phones, and of course, the Internet. As parents we must counter this influence with love, example, and instruction. Otherwise someone else will teach our children about pornography, and the visual aids they might use may be so enticing that they lure our children into a fantasy world full of guilt, shame, and remorse. Pornography is not safe, and we can't assume our kids will never be tempted. Being proactive but not "preachy" or panicked is the best way for helping our kids. As the Scripture says, "Guard your heart above all else, for it determines the course of your life."[4]

Oral Sex

Over the past decade, there has been a significant increase in the proportion of teenagers engaging in oral sex. One four-teen-year-old girl described the attitude of thousands of her peers when she wrote, "Oral sex is not real sex. I would do it to preserve my virginity." A recent study reported that over 54 percent of kids ages fifteen to nineteen say they have had oral sex.[5] This is an alarming, prevalent philosophy that I believe can take a toll on sexual integrity. Even strong Christian kids will say, "We have oral sex because we took a sexual purity pledge and plan on waiting until we are married to have sex."

Oral sex *is* sex. I believe that if you have genital contact, you have had sex. Our sexuality is based on so much more than just intercourse, and this needs to be communicated to kids. Parents need to fight against the cultural norm of "friends with benefits," redefining the practice and letting kids know that no matter how casual they think sexual activity is, it has consequences. For one thing, far too many young people don't realize that oral sex can result in the transmission of sexually transmitted diseases (STDs). Emotional risks are also involved with oral sex.

My general rule of thumb is that we talk with our kids about difficult subjects in a general way early, and then do so again at an age-appropriate time—before they could enter into this kind of behavior. My concern is that far too many parents put off the tough conversations until it is actually too late to make a difference in their child's life.

A young woman wrote me an e-mail after listening to a radio show we did on oral sex. She described her feelings and the consequences young people face better than I can.

> *Dear Jim,*
>
> *Thanks so much for your direct, honest, blunt, and Christian approach to a very delicate subject. Now I wish my mom would have talked to me about this subject. When I was in high school, I got caught up with the raging hormones and curiosity, and I took my eyes off my priorities. I let my then-boyfriend talk me into having oral sex over about an eight-month period. I knew I was violating my values, and I did it anyway. It was self-centered for both of us. The intimacy of oral sex actually seemed more intimate after a while than regular sex, so we compromised our values and did both. Thank God I didn't get pregnant. (We didn't always use birth control.) I do have a sexually transmitted disease from my relationship. Now I am recently married. I love my husband. He was actually a virgin on our wedding night. I know I am forgiven, but the experience with my high school boyfriend still haunts me. I can't get those experiences out of my mind, plus I will live with an STD for the rest of my life. Thanks again for your honesty and for your grace. Jen*

Jen wrote about so many of the concerns I have for this generation. She even mentioned that she wished her mom would have been more direct about talking to her about this subject. Don't assume your child will understand the consequences of oral sex. No doubt this is a very difficult subject to bring up to your children, but if over half of all teens have experienced oral sex by the time they are nineteen years old, we must discuss this important issue no matter how uncomfortable it is for us as parents.

The Physical Consequences

Sometimes the only sex education parents give to their kids is about the physical consequences to sexual promiscuity. Of course, there *are* physical consequences. But remember that for most teens and preteens, they have the "it will happen to someone else" mentality. Also, for many young people, sexual promiscuity is often acted upon spontaneously. This causes even more concern for the physical consequences of unwanted pregnancy and sexually transmitted diseases. On top of that, the statistics are quite serious when it comes to drinking alcohol and then engaging in sexual activity.

Sexually Transmitted Diseases (STDs)

Every year in the United States alone, over twelve million people are infected with an STD. Of those twelve million, close to three million are teenagers. It is one of the more silent epidemics in the world today because an STD brings about shame, and it is simply not often discussed or dealt with properly.

Parents and their kids need to know that a majority of people twenty-five years old and younger who are sexually active will contract an STD, mainly because they usually have more than one partner before they are married. With the growing amount of sexual promiscuity in our culture, this means the STD epidemic will only get worse.

My suggestion is that before your children would ever choose to be sexually active, give them the most up-to-date information on sexually transmitted diseases. There are many excellent Web sites and books on STDs, and any hospital or doctor's office can also give you the latest information. In the meantime, let me briefly assist you with the information that will be helpful to share as you discuss with your child the physical consequences of sexual activity. All these STDs can be passed on through more than just sexual intercourse. With one out of every four teenagers contracting an STD each year, this problem is something we just can't ignore.

About 25 percent of Americans are infected with *genital herpes*. This and other types of the herpes virus can be treated, but there is no known cure. It is important to teach your children that genital herpes can be contracted through oral, anal, or vaginal intercourse.

Chlamydia is a very common sexually transmitted disease. Men carry and can pass on this disease, but it involves much worse risks for women, including possible infertility.

Gonorrhea and *syphilis* are two other common physical consequences of sexual promiscuity. Both STDs can be treated, but they are also known as more of a silent disease at the beginning because there are very few symptoms. You can't treat a disease that you don't know you have.

HIV (human immunodeficiency virus) is the seventh leading cause of death among fifteen- to twenty-four-year-olds. Many parts of the continent of Africa are struggling to survive because of this sexually transmitted disease. Obviously, for non-married young people, the most effective choice to save themselves from this disease is abstinence.

Janet talked to me after a conference. She told me that she was a pastor's kid who had strayed a bit. At a camp one week, she ended up meeting and falling for a boy from another city. She knew he wasn't the best influence, but she wasn't morally perfect either. They ended up having sexual intercourse once. Almost a year later, she found out she had HIV. When she went to tell the boy, he had died of AIDS. She still had not told her parents. She had been worried about unprotected sex and pregnancy, but now she was worried about her life. Although the circumstance may not have changed, she added that her parents had never talked to her about the physical consequences of sexual promiscuity.

Unwanted Pregnancies

Just this week I talked to a young married woman who was very pregnant. These were the happiest days of her life, she said. The expectation of waiting for the new baby was thrilling for her and her husband. What a contrast to when a young woman gets pregnant out of wedlock or when a young man gets someone pregnant. It can be one of the most difficult experiences in life. First, there is often the surprise and pain of finding out, followed by extreme confusion about what the future holds, as well as shame about the circumstances. In nine out of ten cases, the man does not commit to taking care of the woman or the baby. It is a lonely and confusing time, and hard decisions lie ahead.

It's very important for parents to talk with their children, including the young men, about the *results* of pregnancy before there is a pregnancy. Long before our girls could date, we discussed all the issues surrounding an unwanted pregnancy. Our family falls strongly on the pro-life side of the spectrum. Our girls needed to know that if they got pregnant before marriage, we would love them no matter what, and, as a pro-life family, we believe a fetus is a living baby residing in his or her mother's womb. We have always chosen to honor women for not aborting their babies. At the same time, we are very open about the difficulties and often smashed dreams experienced by young single moms.

We also needed to work through the discussion of adoption. Personally, I believe that some of the most courageous and loving acts of life are when a birth mother and birth father realize that another couple would do a better job in raising their unplanned child. From their earliest stages of life, our girls knew that adoption was a gift of God, even if it was necessary because of an unwise choice to be sexually promiscuous.

Raising the child is an option that many young people choose. I strongly believe that it is important for every unmarried person to think through the love, nurture, care, and daily responsibilities a child requires. There are some pretty wonderful stories of young people who became pregnant and made the very courageous decision to raise their child, and they have done a very good job. They grew up quickly, became responsible, and today have a loving home. At the same time, we must allow our children to see that a teenager raising a child is not as glamorous as "playing house." It is the real deal, and responsibilities are huge.

I remember one time speaking at a Christian high school on the subject of sexual abstinence. I figured the students had heard it all before, so instead of a normal presentation, I invited a young woman who had gotten pregnant a few months before graduating from that very school. She brought her two-year-old, and I let the toddler run around the stage (with some supervision!) while I interviewed the young mom. I had never seen a high school assembly so attentive and quiet. They listened as this young woman shared about a typical day in her life, with stories about being up at night with the child, cooking, cleaning, working full time, and living in poverty with very little time for friendships. Some of the students thought the toddler was cute, but the reality of the situation was also put at the forefront of their minds. They figured out quite quickly that teenagers are *not* ready for parenthood.

The Emotional and Spiritual Consequences

There is a variety of emotional and spiritual consequences related to sexual promiscuity. This is difficult to explain to a child who has not entered into sexual temptation yet, or to someone who is being defiant toward God's standards of sexuality. Most kids are experiential learners, so it is usually best to have them talk with a person who has made some poor decisions about their sexuality and can speak from experience. If a person doesn't come to mind in your family or community, call a local crisis pregnancy center and ask if you can talk with someone from the center. I usually suggest that parents have a conversation first with the person you choose to speak with in order to make sure you want your children to hear their story.

Over the past thirty years of doing youth and family ministry and listening to stories of unhappiness over unwise sexual decisions, I would say that regret may be the strongest emotional consequence. Most people who have had a desire to set God-honoring sexual standards but have blown it express regret and remorse for their decisions. Feelings of guilt, shame, and extreme disappointment are also common. Looking back at the situation, they wish they would have made a healthier decision. They feel the spiritual consequences of knowing that they missed the mark on God's standards. Some feel their regret so strongly that it even affects their relationship with their spouse when they get married. I had a mother of three teenagers tell me recently, "I'm forty-seven years old and I still live with the guilt of a high school and a college romance." She added, "It has affected my relationship with my husband and my own self-image. I know God has forgiven me, but I just haven't forgiven myself."

Studies have noted a link between depression and sexual promiscuity. Depression doesn't directly lead to sexual promiscuity or vice versa. However, if a person is depressed, they are more prone to being sexually promiscuous, and if they are sexually promiscuous, they are more prone to depression. Depression is on the rise among young people. At the same time, research shows that kids in middle school and high school are more likely to have sex (unprotected sex, at that) if they are depressed.

As I've said before, there's a fine line in presenting all this information about the consequences of sexual promiscuity to our kids. We want them to see that unwise decisions can be very damaging to our physical, emotional, and spiritual health. At the same time, we want to make sure that we present the good and wonderful side of our sexuality and explain that sex is wonderful and beautiful within the confines of a loving marriage. There is a national news organization that says they present the news in a "fair and balanced" way each night. That's a good approach for us parents as well. It almost comes back to the grace and discipline aspect of parenting. How appropriate, when we bring up the issues of sexual promiscuity, that we make sure we tread lightly, filled with grace, yet give our children an awareness of the potential consequences.

CHAPTER SIX

Sexual Abuse: Prevention and Help

You won't enjoy reading this chapter, but it may be the most important section of this book. Unfortunately, sexual abuse is much more prevalent now than just a generation ago. Most authorities tell us that one out of three young women will be sexually abused by the time they reach their nineteenth birthday, and one out of six men will be sexually abused before age nineteen.

As parents, we have the primary responsibility for our children's well-being, and that means it is our job to help prevent sexual abuse by teaching and training our children about this very important problem in our society. Who would have ever thought this would be an imperative part of our parenting process? With focused time and effort, you can change the odds of your children being hurt in an abusive situation. One of the biggest problems is getting parents to recognize that sexual abuse is a growing problem and that they must be a vital part of its prevention.

When I finished graduate school in Princeton, New Jersey, in the mid-seventies to invest my life in youth and family ministry, it never dawned on me that I would have to deal with so many kids and families struggling with sexual abuse. Sexual abuse happens even in the best of families, and what's even more devastating is that over 80 percent of sexual assaults of children are done by someone they know and trust. The myth that sexual assaults are only done by dirty old men who sneak up on children is mainly just that—a myth. Yes, we must help our kids learn to be extremely discerning with strangers, but at the same time we must teach them how to deal with any kind of inappropriate behavior even from people they know, love, and trust.

Greg and Jackie called me to ask what they should do. Their eight-year-old son had become very depressed. He had been complaining for weeks about nightmares. In the past several months he had reverted to bed-wetting. Their son, who was not a fearful person, was now filled with terror when left with the baby-sitter. He would cling to his parents and behave like a much younger child. I asked about the baby-sitter. They said he was a very responsible high-schooler. "We have known him for five years, and he attends our church," they said. My gut told me that something traumatic had happened for their son to be acting the way he was. I challenged them as I would anyone in this situation to get an assessment from a good counselor. In the first meeting, their son told the counselor that the baby-sitter had made him "do things that I didn't want to do." He went on to tell the counselor that the baby-sitter threatened that if he ever told about "their secret," he would tell his parents what a bad boy he was. Greg and Jackie are very good parents. They trusted the baby-sitter, yet sexual abuse still occurred.

Another person I know, Linda, told me about the time when her daughter was sexually abused by a cousin. At a family gathering, an older cousin had come to visit with his parents, and everyone seemed to be having a great time. Linda didn't know it at the time, but the young man started to tickle and poke at her daughter. The tickling turned to inappropriate touch, but her daughter didn't know for sure if the cousin realized what he was doing. Then he quit it. Later that night, when they were watching a movie in the family room, he sat close with a blanket over them and started to fondle her. She was too embarrassed to tell her parents, but the next time the cousin came to visit, she didn't want to get close to him. Her parents actually punished her for being unfriendly to him. It wasn't until years later that Linda's daughter told her the truth.

The stories could go on and on. They are not easy to tell or hear or live with. They are true stories of emotional and physical pain. What is worse, only one in twenty sexual abuse cases is ever reported. That secret pain makes abuse even more traumatic. Parents can help prevent sexual abuse, but they need to be proactive with information and intentional about prevention.

What Is Sexual Abuse?

Sexual abuse occurs in many forms. Whenever a child is made uncomfortable by another person's sexual behavior or even sexual innuendo, most likely sexual abuse has occurred. When a young person is forced, tricked, or threatened to have sexual contact, abuse has happened. Sexual abuse can be non-contact behaviors like an adult exposing himself or asking a child to look at pornographic materials, or sexual abuse can be physical, ranging from fondling to intercourse to violent rape. In all instances of sexual abuse, the child is being used as an object by the sexual violator. The Internet has changed the way predators can show children pornographic material and even take nude photos of children. This is one of the main reasons why sexual abuse is even more prevalent today.

Russ was a typical thirteen-year-old boy who was intrigued with the World Wide Web. He would frequently tell his mom and dad that he had a new friend in places like Germany, South America, or somewhere else in the U.S. Russ spent lots of time online, chatting and playing video games. His parents had some concerns about his always being on the computer, but they thought it was helping his grades (he was an A-student), and it kept him home and out of trouble. Little did they know that Russ was leading a double life. Somehow he had become hooked up with people who would pay him to undress and do lewd acts in front of the video camera on his computer. One online "friend" had taught Russ how to set up a bank account without his parents' knowledge and a post office box to receive the money. Russ finally got caught—not by his parents, but by an undercover sting operation. Russ's story is a sad but good illustration of a relatively new kind of sexual abuse.

Sexual abuse occurs in all cultural, ethnic, occupational, and socio-economic groups. The headlines in newspapers around the world remind us that sexual abuse sometimes takes place with "good church people." Abusers tend to stay close to children, so we parents need to pay extra attention to anyone who is paying attention to our children. I have worked with kids all of my adult life. The vast majority of people I know who work with children and youth are some of the finest people in the world. But parents still have to keep a watchful eye. I am a big proponent of all youth organizations having criminal checks done on their workers. This won't keep every predator away, but the organization who does fingerprint will bring confidence to parents and put predators on watch that they take sexual abuse seriously.

In another generation, we didn't have to worry about baby-sitters as much. Today, baby-sitters should be interviewed and screened.[1] Cathy and I always asked for references. We chose to pay top-dollar, and it allowed us to keep the best baby-sitters with us for a long time.

As parents, we also need to do what we can about the ever-increasing problem of sexual abuse in dating relationships, most often by boyfriends. Some guys try to control and dominate girls to somehow feel powerful and important, or to be a "real man." Girlfriends sometimes are seen as possessions, and sex is a form of competition (as reflected when guys ask each other,

"Did you score?"). A boyfriend might force his girlfriend to have sex or coerce her in some other way, like saying, "You'd do it if you really loved me."

Your child might be years away from dating, but boys and girls both need to know what are healthy attitudes and behaviors in any guy-girl relationship and what is abuse.

Signs and Signals of Sexual Abuse

Authorities often remind us that parents sometimes go into denial when their child has been sexually traumatized. Instead of standing up for the child, disbelief, shame, a family secret, or some other factor will cause them to resist getting the help the child needs. At the same time, I would caution you to not become an "armchair counselor" and look at every problem your child might be having as a sign of sexual abuse. If you do have any questions or worries, though, it is always better to be on the safe side and get an assessment of the situation from a reputable therapist who has expertise in the area of sexual abuse.

The following list is an introduction to possible signs and symptoms of sexual trauma. It is not meant to be thorough. As I just mentioned, if you have any suspicions, don't suffer in silence; seek help. There are also excellent books and materials available. The presence of an individual sign or symptom in your child does not mean that he or she has been sexually abused, but if you see many of these issues together, you should seek an assessment:

Younger Children

- Bed-wetting
- Sleep disturbances
- Nightmares
- Lack of appetite
- Clinging with a fear of being left alone or with someone they have been alone with
- Depression
- Sexually acting out or sex play with dolls or toys
- Drawing naked pictures
- Acting seductively
- Acts of sexual aggression

Older Children

- Learning problems in school
- Poor peer relationships
- Self-destructive behavior, suicidal, medicating their pain with drug and alcohol abuse
- Nervous, aggressive, disruptive, destructive behavior (perhaps acting out their hurt to secure attention)
- Running away
- Seductive and promiscuous behavior
- Shutting down sexually and emotionally
- Lack of trust and hostility toward authority figures

- Fear of going home, fear of being left alone with the abuser
- Severe depression
- Pain, itching, bleeding, bruises in the genital area
- Extremely low self-esteem

This is just a partial list, and again, it is very normal for most kids to have some of these symptoms and not be sexually abused. However, if many of these symptoms are in their life, then an assessment should be done.

What to Do if Your Child Tells You He or She Has Been Abused

With sexual abuse statistics running so high, there is a chance that a parent's nightmare could come to fruition. Many authorities tell me that they wish parents had a better handle on what to do if their child has been traumatized by sexual abuse. Again, the following information is not meant to take the place of getting the help you need, but it may be a good introduction to what you should do if your child reports being sexually abused.

- *Go with your child to a private place where they will feel comfortable talking.* This is not the time for you to talk or probe, but let them tell you what happened in their own words. Listen with empathy. Listening is a language of love. Let them tell you at their pace. You can ask to clarify issues, but don't drill them. I always tell parents not to show extreme anger toward the perpetrator in front of the kids during the initial conversation. The most important thing you can do is to *believe* your child. Most kids won't lie about it. As you work through the process, experts will help you get the whole story. You are their parent, not a counselor. Imagine walking down the street and someone hitting you in the face with a two-by-four piece of wood. There would be blood and broken bones. When a child is sexually molested, the same feelings take place, but you don't often see the hurt like you would with that two-by-four.

- *Express concern for your child.* Tell them how sorry you are for them and that you will protect them from further molestation. They need assurance that you will care for them and do whatever it takes to get help. Many kids will not want to talk to the police or Child Protective Services. They will need to do this, but make sure they know you will be there for them along the way. This is the time to be supportive and affirming. Give them your time, and don't criticize them. Some parents have missed the mark by making comments like, "That was dumb (or careless)." Provide security and a sense of belonging. Kids need encouragement, and they need to know you care. I tell parents to pray with their children often through this process.

- *Don't think you can handle it alone.* If you suspect your child has any kind of injury, contact your regular physician or go directly to a hospital emergency room.

Recognize that there are medical, emotional, and spiritual needs that experts in the field can address. They can come alongside you and your child and bring hope. You will also need the help of Child Protective Services. Too many parents think they can handle it alone, especially if the abuser is a family member or friend. Let me be very blunt: You can't handle it, and you won't do as good a job as a professional. Think at all times about what is best for your child. The social service system in the United States is not perfect, but Child Protective Services almost always does a good job with help and information. Do not hesitate to call them. (Any counselor, teacher, or youth worker is legally required to report abuse, and that is a good thing.) Don't keep abuse a secret.

What Can You Do to Prevent Sexual Abuse?

Just like teaching your children to look both ways before crossing a street or not to talk with strangers, it's important to teach your children about sexual abuse. You don't want to scare them at too young an age, but you do want to provide security for them with important information. Teach your children that if anyone touches them in a sexual way or does anything that makes them feel uncomfortable, they should report it to you. Help your kids learn that they have the right to say NO if asked to do something that makes them feel uncomfortable, even if the person who asks is a relative or close friend.

Let me remind you that you are in the protection business.

This means you will want to ask baby-sitters for references, pick your kids up from school, and teach your children not to play alone in alleys, empty buildings, or even public rest rooms. It is sad that we have to take these precautions, but this is the world in which we live, and we must make sure they are safe. At the same time, let your children know that they can come to you and talk about anything and you will not judge them.

As our girls became old enough to have even more blunt conversations about sexual abuse, here was the list that Cathy and I created to help them prevent sexual assault or abuse.

- *It's okay to say no.* Don't accept rides, gifts, or favors from strangers. In our home we role-played situations and let our kids practice how to respond. As our girls got older, we helped them understand that no matter what, it was very appropriate to say no to a boyfriend or someone else. *No* is a safe word.

- *If in doubt, stay away.* It's better to be safe than sorry. It's better to do something unpopular than regret making a decision for the sake of wanting to be liked. One of our daughters had an eerie feeling about a dad of someone she was baby-sitting. We encouraged her not to take another baby-sitting job with that family. Again, it is better to be safe than sorry. We have chosen not to let our children ride with people who we know are alcoholics. We don't make a big deal about it; we just don't let it happen.

- *Develop a "report-in" policy.* As a parent, you shouldn't have to guess where your kids might be. We were the "conservative" parents who told our kids from kindergarten on, that if they were going to someone's house, we would always call the parents. When the girls were younger, it was more or less expected, but even in high school, we still made the call. We even established a secret code word our kids could use during phone calls to discreetly alert us of possible trouble. At the sound of that secret word, they knew that we would immediately drop what we were doing and show up wherever they needed us to be.

What I Tell Kids About Sexual Abuse

I have had a most incredible privilege to speak to well over a million students about sex and sexuality. The message over the years about following the Purity Code has pretty much stayed the same, but what has changed is that in every venue, large or small, I now almost always add information about sexual abuse. I seldom used to bring up the subject, but more and more students were coming to me after talks and asking about sexual abuse. Sometimes the situation is presented as "a friend who . . . ."

There is a great deal of pain and confusion among young people who are trying to cope with abuse. And if members of an audience haven't been abused, I assume they know someone who has experienced this trauma. As soon as I transition to speaking about sexual abuse, the room gets very quiet. I watch kids put their heads down. I have seen people run out of auditoriums. I can feel the tension in the room. My message is simple, with four quick points. I go into much greater detail in my book *The Purity Code,* which is written directly to preteens. Here, though, is a brief synopsis:

If you or a friend of yours has been sexually abused . . .

1. *It is not your fault.* Sexual abuse is always the fault of the abuser. Far too many students blame themselves. People who sexually molest and abuse kids are tragically very sick. You are a victim of a crime against you.

2. *Do not suffer in silence; seek help.* Too many people suffer from this trauma in silence. It continues to gnaw away at your life in so many ways, but silence will not bring healing. If one of your friends had cancer but resisted treatment, my guess is that you would beg them to seek help. The same is true of sexual abuse. Those who get help work through their issues. Those who do not seek help often carry their burdens into other relationships and life itself. I know people who have kept their sexual abuse a secret and it hurt their marriage and even their relationship with God. Thousands of people say the best thing (and maybe the hardest thing) they ever did was seek help. I would beg you to seek help.

3. *There is hope!* When someone has been sexually abused, they often are discouraged and lack much hope in the future and in relationships. Sexual abuse is painful in every way,

but people who work through their difficult experience lead wonderful, fulfilling lives. They all have something in common. They took the courageous step to get help.

4. *God cares.* Many people who have been sexually abused blame God. They have a hard time seeing where God fits into the picture. Sexual abuse can and often does distort a person's concept of God. Trusting God as a loving, heavenly Father is a concept that needs to be dealt with spiritually. But the side of God I think of when someone has been abused is the scene captured in the shortest verse of the Bible: "Jesus wept." The context of this Scripture is that Jesus actually cried at the death of a friend. If Jesus wept then, I know He weeps for those who are victims of sexual abuse. He knows and understands your pain, and He wants to come alongside your walk toward healing and wholeness.

This was not an easy chapter to write, and I doubt if you would say it was at all fun to read. However, part of teaching healthy sexuality to our children includes the area of prevention, and preventing sexual abuse is one of the most important instructions we can ever give to our children. Let's pray for God's protection, and that we all do what we can to prevent this traumatic experience and know that there is healing for those who do suffer.

CHAPTER SEVEN

Dealing With
Your Own Sexuality

"If I was sexually active before marriage, should I tell my children?" This question falls under the category of "Always-Asked Questions" anytime I speak to parents on the subject of teaching their children healthy sexuality. Very close to the heart of any communicator is the fact that even if you are talking about someone else, most listeners personalize the topic for their own life. Again, at every session, someone will come to me and say, "I wish I had known this information when I was growing up. It would have made a big difference in my life."

As I have written in previous chapters, many of us did not receive good, healthy, positive sex education from our parents, which makes it more difficult for us to communicate with our children about sexuality. However, another major reason that many parents do not want to talk about sexuality with their kids is because they have fallen short when it comes to their own sexual integrity. It's either too painful, too shameful, or just plain awkward. However, the illustration of the flight attendant who tells adults to put on their own oxygen masks before they help their children works when we think about teaching our children healthy sexuality. We have to take the lead and, frankly, before our children follow the Purity Code, we have to live it first.

Unfortunately, too many parents haven't worked through their own sexuality issues, and it can really hurt their children. They might not still be making huge compromises with their sexuality, but like the woman who asked me if she should share her promiscuous past with her children, they just haven't fully dealt with their past.

To answer her question, though, kids aren't looking for perfect parents; they are looking for people who are authentic with their life, faith, and even their sexuality. I don't think parents need to tell every war story from the past, but sometimes it is helpful to say something like, "I didn't follow the Purity Code at all times, so one of the reasons I am passionate about trying to help you understand God-honoring sexuality is because if you make wise decisions in this area of your life, you will have a better shot at building healthy relationships."

When a person models healthy sexual behavior, their children will be more apt to follow. Let's face it: We were created as sexual beings. God created our sexuality. Sex is sacred, sex is serious, sex is fun, sex is pleasurable, and healthy sexuality is very fulfilling. That is God's idea, not mine. God places a very high value on our sexuality. It's in our very being, and it shouldn't be something to be ashamed of but rather enjoyed and respected. How you view your own sexuality will play a determining factor in how you communicate with your children.

Recently I was talking with a single mom who was deeply concerned about her daughter's behavior with boys. She felt her daughter did not have healthy boundaries. As she talked about her daughter, I could read between the lines that the mother was in an inappropriate relationship with a man as well. She wanted purity for her daughter but she wasn't willing to make the same decision she was asking of her fifteen-year-old. My input ended up not focusing on her daughter but on her. I wish I could tell you that the mother agreed with me, but she didn't. Basically she saw no correlation between her lifestyle and what she wanted for her daughter. My guess is that the girl will follow her mom's example. Children see, children do.

You First

You will have to work on your own healthy sexuality before you help your children. This doesn't mean you will lead a perfect life or have a perfect past, but the people who seem to do the best are the people who ruthlessly deal with their own brokenness and "repair" the past. These people are very intentional about creating a more intimate marriage. They practice fidelity and purity in their own lives, and they seek forgiveness as well as give forgiveness.

Be ruthlessly honest about your own brokenness. If you had unhealthy experiences in the past or are struggling with issues today relating to sexuality, or anything else for that matter, deal with them. If you need counseling, then call today. If there is an experience that seems to hold you back, work on it beginning today. The Bible is clear: "Where there is no counsel, the people fall; but in the multitude of counselors there is safety" (Proverbs 11:14 NKJV). When it comes to our sexuality, though, we tend to repress or ignore hurts and pain. The issues will seep out of our lives in other ways, and I believe this often hinders our children from looking at their own sexuality in a healthy manner. If something in your life is broken or holding you back, do what you can to fix it.

Create intimacy in your marriage. Intimacy isn't just about a physical and sexual relationship. Intimacy is more about connection. A study by University of Washington marriage authority Dr. John Gottman found that emotional connection was the missing element in marriages that ended in divorce. If there is no emotional intimacy or connection in your own marriage, there will be little interest in true sexual intimacy. Keeping the spark alive in your own marriage will actually enhance your ability to connect with your children on the right kind of level. A poor or loveless marriage can create a negative family environment. Keep working on your relationship. Don't let your kids spoil your romance. Keep learning about your sexuality. The more comfortable you are with your marital intimacy, the easier it will be to have healthy sexuality conversations with your kids.

Creating an intimate marriage will be a most positive force in your family. I love Paul's advice written in Romans 12:10, "Outdo one another in showing honor" (ESV).

Practice fidelity and purity. The road to healthy sexuality, as well as emotional and physical intimacy, is through the gate of fidelity and purity. Pornography is a growing problem in American homes. The porn industry often leads the way on the Web. There are hundreds of new sites each week. Porn revenue is larger than all the professional football, basketball, and baseball franchises put together, and it exceeds the combined revenues of the CBS, ABC, and NBC television networks.[1] More than thirty-eight million Americans regularly visit Internet porn sites.[2] Today there are more divorces caused by porn addiction than ever before. You simply can't have a healthy sense of sexuality and be involved with porn, period.

The same goes for emotional affairs. An emotional affair is spending time thinking about being with someone other than your spouse. When you dress, do you keep in mind how that other person will like your outfit? Do you have private conversations with someone of the opposite sex that you wouldn't have with your own spouse? Have you said or done anything that is inappropriate with that person? Even an emotional affair can block healthy intimacy with your spouse.

Seek forgiveness/give forgiveness. Jenny had never forgiven herself for some of her past shortcomings. She constantly beat herself up emotionally because of some bad decisions made years ago. As a Christian she understood that God had forgiven her, but she couldn't forgive herself. Finally, Jenny realized that it was a bit arrogant of her to seek God's forgiveness and yet not forgive herself.

Forgiveness and grace are very powerful experiences that can free you up to move toward healthy sexuality. Sometimes you have to seek forgiveness and other times you have to give forgiveness. Both experiences bring healing and joy in relationships. We were not meant to live in bitterness and resentment. Jesus said, "You will know the truth and the truth will set you free." Working the steps toward forgiveness brings freedom, and freedom allows you to be healthier in your sexuality. You win, your spouse wins, and eventually your kids win.

Setting Boundaries

Over the years I have watched some really good people make some very poor choices involving their sexuality. They didn't set up healthy boundaries, and they found themselves compromising their values. They didn't start out to have an affair or lose their marriage. The last thing on their minds was that their decisions would affect their children, but their decisions did change the family dynamic.

Mark and Becky were good friends of ours. We met when our children were on the same gymnastics team. We had dinner together several times and really enjoyed each other's company.

One day Becky called my office and asked if she could come

in and talk. So far, our relationship had only been through our kids, and I didn't even know that she understood what I did for a living. I invited her to come and talk that very day. When she walked through my office door I could tell she had been crying. She sat down and blurted out that Mark had been having an affair with a woman from his work. Mark traveled a bit with his job, and Becky had a funny feeling about the amount of time he was spending with this co-worker. She confronted him and his story unfolded.

In the busyness of life, Becky had put all her best energy into the kids' lives and her at-home business. Mark had complained about feeling ignored many times. He didn't help much because he was also busy at work and trying to be a good father. They were neglecting their marriage. What was once a burning, passionate relationship was now more like a business relationship focused on raising three kids and talking about the mortgage and insurance. A couple of years of neglect in the marriage had caused Mark and Becky to drift apart.

Mark loved Becky, but at work he found someone who genuinely seemed interested in him. This woman didn't know his kids or Becky, but she took the time to look at pictures of the family and listen to Mark brag about the kids' activities. She had mentioned to him in passing that she had a tough marriage with a husband who drank too much. Mark began to find excuses to spend more and more time with this other woman. At first the relationship was not sexual; Mark knew where an affair would lead and he didn't want to risk losing his wife and kids.

Mark felt lost but didn't know anyone he could talk to. Before long, he had become emotionally and physically involved with the other woman. Mark was torn. In many ways he wanted out of the affair and back into a loving relationship with his wife, but in his guilt and shame he found more reasons to withdraw. By the time Becky confronted him, their relationship was an emotional shell with little depth. They were together at games, school activities, church, and even had some moments of intimacy, but most nights they would sleep six inches apart from each other but miles apart emotionally.

Becky knew she was partly to blame for the neglect and the drifting. The kids were needy and took most of her attention. Mark was at a stage in his life where he wanted to try to heal the relationship, but Becky wasn't sure. She was wounded and hurting. The kids didn't know the whole story, but they knew something was obviously wrong.

Though I changed the names and some of the circumstances recounted in this story, it happens every day in thousands of homes. A marriage is compromised, the children are hurt, and the pain is deep.

As much as I wanted to help put Mark and Becky's relationship back together, I also wanted to ask the question, "How did you get to this place, and what could you have done to keep from going down that road?" In the end, what they needed, especially Mark, was personal discipline and boundaries. A constant phrase with my own children and life is, "It's either the pain of discipline, or the pain of regret." Developing healthy boundaries is a real source of discipline. Let's look for a moment at what Mark could have done to stay away from compromising behavior.

Accountability is one of the basic needs of men and woman. Too many people live their lives isolated and unwilling or unable to share their life with anyone. I remember the day I heard on the radio that a well-known leader, a mentor of mine, had fallen morally with an affair. I was at a conference speaking with my good friend Dr. Henry Cloud, the coauthor of the bestselling book *Boundaries*. I remember asking Henry, "What do you think went wrong?" His answer: "I'll bet he had no accountability." As I got to know the situation, Henry was absolutely right.

In order to have healthy boundaries with the opposite sex, we need the accountability of others who have access to our soul. Every Tuesday morning I meet with four men. We study the Bible together, share life issues, and support one another. This accountability group makes me a better husband and more effective father.

There are times when it is embarrassing to share a struggle with someone, but with accountability we can keep ourselves from making unwise decisions. This book is dedicated to a friend of mine, Jon Wallace, who is the president of Azusa Pacific University. We have known each other for years, but over the past decade we have grown to respect and appreciate each other through an accountability relationship. There are times when we get together and grade our priorities. I would drop whatever I was doing to be with Jon if he needed me, and I find that a deep friendship like ours comes out of an intentional accountability relationship.

We need to be able to answer questions like:

- Am I being faithful to my calling and my priorities?
- Have I done anything since our last visit that was inappropriate in mind or deed with the opposite sex?
- Am I being faithful to my commitment to Cathy?
- Am I being faithful to my commitment to my children?
- Do I spend my money wisely and with stewardship?
- Am I faithful to my spiritual disciplines?
- Have I lied to Jon to make him think more highly of me?

In all honesty, sometimes these are not easy questions to answer. However, these are the accountability-type questions that will bring healthy boundaries to our lives. In Mark and Becky's case, Mark could have used an honest relationship with some men who would have understood his schedule and helped him stay on course, but instead Mark was an island unto himself, and no one knew of his intense struggle.

Guarding your heart, your mind, and your eyes is another boundary discipline. The answer to this boundary situation is found in the great Proverb "Guard your heart above all else, for it determines the course of your life."[3] This guarding relates to the discipline of viewing habits, reading, and Internet use, as well as the discipline of not allowing our heart to move in a direction that would be hurtful to our marriage. It is the same principle we use when we tell our children, "If you put garbage into your life, garbage comes out." For men, the garbage is often visual. They really do have a problem with their eyes and mind. Women tend to be more emotionally involved.

Recently on a radio program, I heard the story of a man and woman whose fourteen-year-old daughter was stalked by a much older sexual predator. Theirs is a very difficult story of a man flying across state lines to have sex with their daughter, who later took her own life. The man first got involved after seeing some compromising photographs of the fourteen-year-old. The girl eventually was seduced by his words of affirmation and understanding. She thought she had found her soul mate on the Internet. Tragically, it was all a lie.

We must guard our hearts and lives from thoughts and experiences that stain our souls. For me, that means being intentional about asking myself questions like:

- Do I like the human being I am becoming?
- Is my heart for God growing or shrinking?
- Am I only giving my family my emotional scraps?
- Have I allowed compromising material or relationships to enter my mind, eyes, or heart?

If I don't like the answers, then I need to immediately and openly talk with my accountability partners and with my wife, Cathy.

Healthy boundaries with the opposite sex take intentionality. I wish we lived in a world where it was simple to have friends of the opposite sex and not face the temptation of losing our way. Unfortunately, no one is that strong. It takes intentionality and boundaries. I have several friends who are women. I love them and respect them, but I also know that in order to keep the relationship healthy, I need to set good boundaries. For example, I don't have a private lunch with someone of the opposite sex. There are times this has made a woman frustrated from a business standpoint, but nevertheless, the boundary is a good one. As a person who travels and speaks, I also ask that a woman does not pick me up at an airport alone. This doesn't mean that the moment I would get in a car with a woman, bad things could happen. Because of my visibility in the Christian community, however, even the appearance of a compromising situation can cause a doubt in someone's mind. Dr. Billy Graham chose to never even be in an elevator alone with a woman. If one person made a negative accusation about him with a lie, his ministry could have been stained.

I think most people do fall into infatuation with someone of the opposite sex, even those in a good marriage. Still, healthy boundaries will keep the relationship on the pure side. It really is a constant guarding of the heart. If you find yourself dreaming about what it would be like to be with another person or sharing very personal, intimate conversation with someone of the opposite sex who is not your spouse, then you are on the way toward an emotional affair.

Some people will think I have gone too far with some of these viewpoints. But once again, "Better safe than sorry." If I can treat a woman with a healthy respect and honor her as a cherished sister, I will avoid unhealthy, painful relationships that get in the way of creating an intimate marriage or being a good role model for my children. It all goes back to the pain of discipline or the pain of regret. There is pain in both situations, but the pain of discipline is much healthier for all.

CHAPTER EIGHT

Questions and Answers

In many of my speaking sessions on the subject of healthy sexuality, I allow fifteen to twenty minutes for questions and answers. I usually use all that time and more. Often I am the last to leave an auditorium because the subject tends to involve personal questions and issues.

When it comes to teaching your children about healthy sexuality, there are no bad questions. Unfortunately, because of space constraints, my answers here might not be as thorough as you would have hoped. I would encourage you to pose any questions you might have to experts in your local area. If you have trouble finding a good resource, do not hesitate to write the HomeWord staff (Contactus@HomeWord.com), who will be glad to give you their input or referrals.

You may disagree with some of my answers in this chapter.

I just ask you to remember that addressing a question in a short few paragraphs is not as effective as a personal conversation. Use these answers as a catalyst for further dialogue or reading on the subject.

1. **My parents never talked to me about sex and sexuality. I am not trained in this field, and I have no idea when to talk with my kids and what to tell them. Can you help me?**

Keep your child's developmental stage in the forefront of your mind. I was a bit more specific in chapter 4. You don't feed a baby a large piece of steak, so don't give your children too detailed information before they can comprehend it. At the same time, most parents don't talk enough about sex and sexuality with their kids. Cliff and Joyce Penner are two of my favorite guests on my radio program. They are the authorities I go to for questions on sexuality. Cliff has a PhD in clinical psychology and Joyce is a registered nurse and a clinical nurse specialist. They both specialize in helping people deal with their sexuality from a clinical and Christian point of view. They have a wonderful handout on your question, called Mastering Sexual Development.[1] This handout has been helpful to me, and it's what I pass out to people who ask your question.

Mastering Sexual Development

Stage	Critical Learning	Impact on Sexual Adjustment
Infancy	Bonding	Capacity for intimacy
Toddlerhood	Touching, naming, & control of genitals	Positive acceptance of genitals
Preschool	Question-asking	Open communication about sex
School Age	Exploring	Sexual awareness with boundaries and without shame
Pre-Adolescence	Erotic feelings and bumbling discovery	Self-acceptance and competence in relating to opposite sex
Adolescence	Decision-making	Accept feelings; control actions
Single Adulthood	Becoming whole; developing all forms of intimacy	Ability for intimate bond with opposite sex
Married Adulthood	Giving and receiving of sexual pleasure	Sexual responsiveness and responsibility
Older Adulthood	Adapting to the changes of aging	Slow, pleasure-oriented sex

2. What is your opinion of talking with children about birth control?

As you know from reading this book, I am absolutely, unequivocally *pro-abstinence* before marriage. I believe the Bible is clear about this issue, and I believe the less baggage someone brings into a marriage the better. Sexually intimate relationships before marriage do not enhance a marriage. You may want to ask your pastor if your church has a philosophy on this issue. For example, the Roman Catholic church does not encourage most types of birth control even for married couples.

Your question is actually one that is debated in some circles. Let me give you both views and then you can decide how to handle it. Some very reputable authorities say that under no circumstance would they ever tell their children about birth control. Even if a child admits to being sexually intimate with his or her boyfriend or girlfriend, they would not discuss birth control. They believe that if you give your children information, they may see this as condoning the behavior. On the other hand, there are other authorities who would say that if your child is going against the will of God and having sexual intercourse, you should help them think through practicing birth control for the sake of the possible unborn child. The whole birth control issue is a difficult one to discern, and yet I believe it is extremely important for you to have an open conversation with your kids about your belief on this matter sometime around fourteen or fifteen years of age, or for some children even younger.

3. Should I allow my children to attend the sex education classes in their public school?

It is definitely the job of the parents to take the lead in the sex education of their children. This may be the strongest theme in this book. However, you may be surprised to hear from me that I am not totally opposed to sex education in schools. Here is what Cathy and I did when our youngest daughter was in middle school. First, we attended a parents' information night. There were seven parents, including ourselves, from a school of over a thousand kids. We met the teachers, looked over the curriculum, and asked questions. Although this was not a Christian school, both teachers had very similar values to our own. We were even invited to attend the class with our daughter or attend another class at a different time period. We didn't do it, but we have often encouraged parents to attend a class other than their child's. (Most middle school kids would rather drink poison than have their parents be in a sex education class with them.)

At the school my daughter attended, there was a series of sex education and family life classes. After each session, we took our daughter out for frozen yogurt and discussed that particular topic. Sometimes the conversation was a dialogue and sometimes it was merely her reporting on the subject and our making comments to her. In general, sex was not a topic she cherished bringing up to the parental units! This particular public school stayed away from controversial topics, and we used the classes as a way to continue our discussions on healthy sexuality. You may have a different viewpoint and even a different experience at your public school. I have heard some very strange and horrible stories about how sex education has been presented in public schools, and I would not have wanted my children in those classrooms. I think that is the exception these days, and not the norm. However, it is your job to check out the curriculum, talk with the teachers, and then dialogue with your child. You are in charge of teaching value-based sex education.

4. My daughter thinks I'm old-fashioned because I won't let her participate in a girl/guy sleepover after a school function. She thinks that because it is chaperoned by the parents and in the home of a friend, it is okay. What is your take on girls and guys sleeping overnight together?

Your daughter would call me old-fashioned too. When my girls asked (and they did), Cathy and I went to great lengths to let kids stay late at our home, have fun food, and make it a special occasion, but at a certain time it was time to let the guys stay somewhere else. We weren't necessarily popular with our children at the moment, but they quickly forgot and moved on to the next drama!

I am saddened that parents allow their children to rent hotel rooms or have keg parties after school functions. What are they thinking? Those issues are a no-brainer for me to say no to. The more difficult situation is when someone from our church invites the boys and girls over after the big event for a sleepover. I know there probably won't be alcohol or drugs there, and I'm pretty sure the parents won't allow the guys and girls to sleep in the same room. Nevertheless, it sets a precedent for an experience that may not be as well chaperoned, and it's a marker of behavior that is set at an early age.

You aren't running a popularity contest in situations like this. My favorite line with my own kids was, "I can understand how you feel, and I might have felt the same way when I was your age; NEVERTHELESS, it's not going to happen." Feel their pain, empathize, and then stand your ground!

5. Homosexuality is a lightning rod at my son's school and even at church. My son is not sure what to believe, and he has a friend who says he thinks he might be gay. What would you say to this young man?

The homosexual issue has become much more prevalent in the media as well as on school campuses. And you are absolutely right about it being a lightning rod. The Christian community has not always handled this issue very well. Some leaders have basically said "homosexuals are going to hell," and then we wonder why people who struggle with gender identity don't feel welcomed at our churches. My theology on homosexuality is conservative. I believe the Bible is quite clear that a sexual relationship is meant for a man and a woman who are married. For those who believe that the Bible is the Word of God, it's extremely difficult to believe that homosexuality is not sin. Sin means to miss the mark. Practicing homosexuality misses the mark. The issue is volatile and people get upset. Not everyone agrees on all matters concerning gender confusion, but we must find room to communicate.

My concern is for the young man you wrote me about. He

is experiencing what about 10 percent of the student population today will struggle with at one time or another, and that is gender identity confusion. There are a myriad of reasons why someone might experience an intense confusion about his sexual identity. He may need to differentiate between same-sex attraction and outright homosexual behavior. I always suggest that people open up the conversation and whenever possible create a safe and healthy environment, free from teasing and joking about the topic. Kids who are struggling with gender confusion haven't made up their minds yet, and I believe we need to be there to give them truth, grace, love, and help.

Here's what I think we can do for those who have sexual identity issues: (1) do everything in the light of God's Word and God's love; (2) introduce positive role models; (3) teach kids the scriptural perspective on healthy sexuality and the Purity Code; (4) find ways to address the issue of possible sexual abuse (a majority of gender-confused kids have been sexually abused in one way or another); (5) note possible hormonal problems and help them seek a medical evaluation; and (6) encourage openness and loving dialogue.

I would also suggest that you learn all you can about the facts surrounding homosexual behavior. The following is not meant to be all-informative, but here is what I am concerned about, condensed into one paragraph:

Homosexual behavior is a high-risk lifestyle and can be life threatening. Besides being associated with a greater risk of AIDS (compared with a heterosexual lifestyle), a homosexual lifestyle is also marked by increased alcohol abuse, marijuana use, and cocaine use. The percentage of homosexual men and women who attempt suicide is much higher as well.[2] As I mentioned before, sexual abuse can be a key factor, and some studies say that as much as 80 percent of homosexual men and 70 percent of homosexual women have been sexually abused. In addition to abuse, more homosexuals suffer from sexual addictions than heterosexuals. My point is that the young man you mentioned in your question is facing some very difficult choices that perhaps he hasn't thought about for his life. Obviously he will have to deal with what Scripture says, and he will need love, care, and yes, even understanding to make good choices.

6. My daughter is fifteen and "in love" with a twenty-year-old boy. I like the boy and I don't think they are having an inappropriate sexual relationship, but I wonder about the age difference. Do you think I should have some concerns?

Yes, I do. I'm concerned that a fifteen-year-old is already in an exclusive dating relationship. I'm concerned that a twenty-year-old likes your fifteen-year-old daughter. I'm also concerned that you haven't stepped in and dealt with this relationship. A parent's job is not to make their children happy, but rather help them become responsible adults. I would not let a fifteen-year-old be in a serious relationship with someone who is out of high school and in another developmental stage in life. Let's pretend for a moment that he is a nice guy and doesn't have impure motives. What attracts him to your daughter? Age differences when a couple is in their twenties aren't so pronounced as the teenage years.

Your daughter is learning how to relate to the opposite sex, and the most positive way to do that is relate to boys her age. Of course, not every young man is a predator. He could indeed be a nice young man, but his life experience and life stage is different from your daughter's. Personally, I would try to lovingly end this relationship.

7. My son (age fourteen) told me that he has discovered masturbation. I am a single mom who has no idea how to deal with this situation. What would you suggest and what do you tell other parents?

I am very impressed that your son was willing to talk with you about the issue of masturbation. This proves to me that you have a trusting, safe relationship. Here is the deal: Masturbation is another of those controversial subjects. Some of my favorite authorities have different opinions. I once heard a family expert say, "Ninety-two percent of all boys have the experience of masturbation, and perhaps the other 8 percent may be lying." He meant it for a bit of a laugh, but his statistics might be right on; the vast majority of boys (and more and more girls) have had a self-stimulating sexual experience by the time they graduate from high school. In other words, your son needs to know he is not alone and it is a somewhat normal experience.

My worry with masturbation is that with the incredible increase of Internet pornography among young people, it can lead to obsessive-compulsive behavior, sexual addiction, and worse. The words of Jesus are clear, "But I tell you that anyone who looks at a woman lustfully has already committed adultery with her in his heart" (Matthew 5:28). This Scripture, of course, goes back to building a theology of healthy sexuality. We want to help our children make decisions in line with their purity code.

Many kids today struggle with masturbation as a way of coping with stress. I had a seventeen-year-old woman tell me at a conference that every time she got into an argument with her mother, she would go into her room and masturbate. This was not as much a sexual issue as a way of dealing with her anger in an unhealthy manner.

Some kids need the assistance of an accountability relationship with a parent, friend, or youth worker to help them make better decisions about this issue. There is much more openness today about discussing masturbation, and personally, I think this is a positive sign. Whether it is with you or someone else you and your son trust, he will need to talk about his feelings and concerns. I find that in a single-parent home, it usually rests on the person who the child lives with most of the time. In a two-parent home, I vote a majority of time for the conversation(s) to take place with the same-sex parent.

8. **I know today many people live together instead of getting married. We have friends and relatives who have chosen this lifestyle. I'm afraid as my children get older that they will choose to follow the example of**

these people and live together without getting married. What do you think?

I am very concerned at the incredibly huge increase of people choosing to live together before or instead of getting married. Besides going against the clear scriptural principles in the Purity Code, there are many other reasons to be concerned. Secular social science research overwhelmingly supports marriage over cohabitation. People who live together before marriage tend to break up more than people who don't. Marriage vows tend to serve as the glue that holds the relationship together and obviously provide the most stability for children in the family. Studies show that marriage creates physically healthier individuals and happier people. People who live together will experience at least a four-times-higher rate of infidelity. Those are just some of the facts.

Your model of a marriage of fidelity and faithfulness will be the strongest example for your children's decisions. Teach your children from a young age the Purity Code and, because "more is caught than taught," show them healthy role models. When Cathy and I were first married, only about one million people were in "unmarried households." Today the number is well over twelve million.[3] It is time for us to buck this trend and change it one family at a time. My hunch is that as we see the trend lessen, we will see the divorce rate also go down and the rates of fulfilling marriages go up.

9. The headlines have indicated that having kids take a purity pledge doesn't work. They say it increases the

chance of STDs and only delays sexual intercourse by eighteen months. Do you agree with this?

Millions of courageous young people have walked down the aisles at youth rallies and signed "True Love Waits" abstinence pledges. Others have signed purity pledges in Sunday school, youth group, or better yet, as their parents were teaching them about value-centered sexuality. The pledges vary—some focus on remaining pure until marriage, while the Purity Code encourages a broader perspective: *"In honor to God, my family, and my future spouse, I commit my life to sexual purity."*

Since 2004, the secular headlines have screamed that sexual purity pledges don't work and put kids more at risk for pregnancy and STDs. Are the articles right? I don't think so.

It is true that the National Longitudinal Study of Adolescent Health (which these headlines often quote) revealed some alarming findings. And while many believe the study authors—Hannah Brueckner of Yale University and Peter Bearman of Columbia University—severely misled the press on this subject when the results came out, no one denies that many young people who sign the pledge cards do struggle with keeping their commitment until marriage. The Brueckner/Bearman study found:

- For those who made abstinence pledges, there is about an eighteen-month delay in sexual activity, after which many do succumb to sexual temptation.

141

- Fewer pledgers will use a form of protection from pregnancy and HIV during their first sexual intercourse experience.[4]

Both of these findings are obviously of great concern to those like me, who believe that a commitment to biblical sexuality involves waiting until marriage to have sexual intercourse. It means there is still much more to do than passing out pledge cards to help young people make right and wise decisions about their sexuality. Parents need to be more involved in sex education and help their children develop a strong theological foundation for their decision to wait until marriage to have sexual intercourse. It means teaching young people the biblical truth about sex, that God created sex and He sees it as wonderful in the context of marriage. This is obviously the reason I wrote this book and the entire PURE FOUNDATIONS series.

On the Brighter Side

Robert Rector and Kirk Johnson, of the Heritage Foundation, examined the same study and found contradictions as well as other input that is much more positive and can help spread some light on the negative headlines. They found these facts from within the study as they compared non–pledging adolescents with those who have made a virginity pledge:

- Youth who make virginity pledges are less likely to engage in risky sexual behaviors as young adults

- They are less likely to engage in vaginal intercourse
- They are less likely to engage in oral or anal sex
- They are less likely to engage in sex with or act as prostitutes[5]

Dr. Richard Ross, one of the cofounders and international spokesperson of the incredible worldwide True Love Waits movement, put it this way:

> From the 1970s through 1993, educators, church leaders and even parents seemed to assume most teenagers would be sexually active. Their only challenge to the young was to protect themselves. Teenagers fulfilled their expectations, and rates of sexual activity rose each year. In 1993, the experiences of one church youth group exploded into an international movement in only weeks. Church leaders and parents linked arms to call teenagers to God's very best related to sexuality and purity. Again, the teenagers fulfilled their high call and expectations. For twelve unbroken years, rates of teenage sexual activity have plummeted. But leaders and parents must not become complacent. The pull of a dying culture is great on the young. The moment the clear call to purity becomes muted, the pendulum will begin to swing the other way.[6]

That's why I believe every family and every church needs to challenge kids to purity. The culture assumes that kids are going to be involved in sexual behavior, but studies reveal that the more positive, healthy sex education kids receive from their parents, the less promiscuous they will be.[7]

All of this may be more information than needed for a question about the effectiveness of a purity pledge. However, the way I see it, trying to live by a purity pledge is better than nothing, and whenever parents get involved with teaching healthy sexuality, kids make better decisions.

CHAPTER NINE

Discussion Starters and Faith Conversations

As I have said before, teaching healthy sexuality is more about dialogue than monologue. Kids learn best when they talk, not just when you talk. All of the material in this book and other resources in the PURE FOUNDATIONS series is specifically written from an age-developmental approach and intended to help you keep up a continual dialogue with your kids as they grow up.

As written, the twenty-five discussion starters and faith conversations in this chapter lean toward older kids, but you as the parent will need to decide what is or isn't appropriate for the age of your child. You'll notice that the conversation starters are not geared so much for right and wrong answers but lean toward "I feel" or "my opinion is" answers. Open-ended questions let children know you are willing to listen and dialogue. At the same time, using questions like these provides the opportunity to express your opinions on these important topics. They will want to hear what you have to say, but if it is "preachy" or done in a negative manner, their spirits can be closed very easily.[1]

Discussion Starters

1. Terri made a commitment to sexual purity when she was twelve. Now she is sixteen and has fallen in love with Jason. Terri is rethinking her commitment because she is "in love and it won't hurt anyone to be sexually active." She also believes she will probably marry Jason when they get older. What advice would you give Terri?

2. At what age do you think it is okay to have a boyfriend or a girlfriend?

3. For the parents: Talk about your first date with your child's other parent. How did you meet each other? What did you do on your first date?

4. What would be the ultimate date? What is a good age to start dating or courting?

5. Read 1 Corinthians 13:4–7. What are some of the characteristics of a healthy, loving relationship?

6. Together, brainstorm some of the consequences to an unhealthy relationship with the opposite sex.

7. What would an appropriate hug look like and what would an inappropriate hug look like? If you believe someone gave you an inappropriate hug or made you feel uncomfortable in any way, what would be a good thing to do?

8. If a friend wants to show you pornography on the Internet, what can you say and do?

9. For the parents: What was the best advice you ever received about relating to the opposite sex? What is a poor example of relating to the opposite sex on TV, movies, or the Internet?

10. Your best friend confides in you that they are viewing bad stuff on the computer almost every day. What advice would you give them?

11. True or False
    A. **T or F** The Bible is old-fashioned and out-of-date on the subject of sexuality.
    B. **T or F** The Bible says sex is very good.
    C. **T or F** It is okay to kiss passionately on the first date.
    D. **T or F** Abortion is wrong.
    E. **T or F** Sexual abuse affects one out of three girls by age nineteen.
    F. **T or F** Watching sexual images on TV or in movies does not affect our behavior.
    G. **T or F** It is always a good idea to think about opposite-sex relationships with God's plan for your life in mind.

12. Discussion Topics: Listed below are general topics related to sex, sexuality, and relationships. Think of your child and plan or estimate the appropriate age you'll talk about each topic. Remember there are levels of conversation that can go on at various developmental stages.

_____ Appropriate touch and inappropriate touch

_____ What the Bible says about sex and sexuality

_____ What happens at puberty

_____ Changes going on in your body

_____ Sexual organs

_____ Emotions

_____ Boy/girl attraction

_____ Infatuation vs. real love

_____ Masturbation

_____ Pornography

_____ Sexual abuse, harassment, and teasing

_____ Sexual intercourse

_____ Virginity

_____ Why wait?

_____ Dangers of premarital sexual relationships

_____ Abstinence and purity including the Purity Code

_____ How far is too far?

_____ Homosexuality

_____ AIDS

_____ Lust

_____ Peer pressure

_____ Clothing and modesty

_____ Partying

_____ Movies, music, TV, and Internet influences

_____ See many other topics listed in chapter 4

13. What do you like about your physical appearance? What don't you like about your physical appearance?

14. Question for parents: What makes it uncomfortable at times to discuss subjects like sex and sexuality with your child? Question for children: Do you feel like your parent(s) are open and safe to talk with about sex and sexuality? Why or why not?

15. What in your mind is an appropriate way to dress? What is an inappropriate way to dress?

16. How is grace and forgiveness a part of our lives with relationships?

17. How does the culture influence our sexuality?

18. A group of elementary-aged kids decides to play the game Spin the Bottle. Do you think this "game" is appropriate in elementary school? (Place a mark by the phrase that is closest to what you believe):

_____ Way too young to play this game

_____ It is not an appropriate game at any age

_____ Not sure

19. During a very private conversation, one of your best friends confides in you that a baby-sitter fondled them

inappropriately a year ago. It still seems to bother them, but they don't want you to tell anyone. What would you do?

Faith Conversations:

20. Read Genesis 2:18–25. What do you learn about sexuality from this Scripture?

21. Read Exodus 20:14. Why do you think God included this verse as one of the Ten Commandments?

22. Read 1 Thessalonians 4:3. What are reasons the Bible would say that it is "God's will for us to avoid sexual immorality"?

23. Read 1 Thessalonians 4:3. (Again!) Discuss together what sexual immorality includes.

24. Read Matthew 19:4–6. How do these words that Jesus said, quoting from the Old Testament, relate to our sexuality?

25. Read 1 Corinthians 6:18–20. What are the key points of this Scripture? What does it mean when it says your body is the temple of the Holy Spirit? How can we honor God with our body?

Notes

Chapter One

1. Walt Larimore and Susan Crocket, *The Honeymoon of Your Dreams* (Ventura, CA: Regal Books, 2007), 48–50.

2. *www.kff.org/womenshealth/upload/3040-03.pdf* and *www.cdc.gov/mmwr/PDF/SS/SS5505.pdf*.

3. Jim Burns *10 Building Blocks for a Happy Family* (Ventura, CA: Regal Books, 2003), 50.

Chapter Two

1. Gary and Barbara Rosberg with Ginger Kolbaba, *The 5 Sex Needs of Men and Women* (Carol Stream, IL: Tyndale, 2006), 18.

2. Ray E. Short, *Sex, Love, or Infatuation: How Can I Really Know?* (Minneapolis: Augsburg Publishing House, 1990), 83.

3. Ibid., 83, 88–89.

Chapter Three

1. Hayley DiMarco, *Technical Virgin* (Grand Rapids: Revell, 2006), 9.

2. Hayley DiMarco, *Sexy Girls: How Hot Is Too Hot?* (Grand Rapids: Revell, 2006), 89.

3. For information on how I would talk to kids about some of these subjects, see my book *Accept Nothing Less: God's Best for Your Body, Mind, and Heart* (Minneapolis: Bethany House, 2008).

4. Fred Stoeker and Stephen Arterburn, *Every Man's Battle* (Colorado Springs: Waterbrook Press, 2000), 125.

5. Ibid., 131.

6. DiMarco, *Sexy Girls: How Hot Is Too Hot?*, 105.

7. Stephen Arterburn and Jim Burns, *How to Talk to Your Kids About Drugs* (Eugene, OR: Harvest House, 2007).

Chapter Four

1. Some of the topics covered are listed in chapter 1.

2. Much more of this rite-of-passage blessing is discussed in my book *Confident Parenting* in chapter 7, "The Lesson of the Blessing: Bringing Security and Honor to Your Home."

3. For my suggestion on how to walk through puberty basics with your kids, see my book *The Purity Code.*

Chapter Five

1. Examples of Internet filters: *www.CommonSenseMedia.org, www.WebWiseKids.org, www.SafeTeens.com, www.GetWise*

.com, *www.iSafe.org, www.BlogSafety.com, www.Software 4Parents.com, www.SafeEyes.com.*

2. Jolene L. Roehlkepartin, *Parents of Teenagers,* "The Lure of MTV," December 1991/January 1992.

3. Recommended book: Stephen Arterburn and Roger Marsh, *Internet-Protect Your Kids* (Nashville: Thomas Nelson, 2007).

4. Proverbs 4:23 NLT

5. C. Birnbaum, "The Love and Sex Survey 2000," Twist magazine, October/November 2000.

Chapter Six

1. More tips for finding trustworthy baby-sitters include: (1) church youth groups are often good places to find baby-sitters, but due diligence is still needed; (2) most baby-sitting agencies have excellent reference checks; (3) trade baby-sitting with parents you trust.

Chapter Seven

1. Stephen Arterburn and Jim Burns, *Parents' Guide to Top 10 Dangers Teens Face* (Wheaton, IL: Tyndale, 1995), 224.

2. *http://abcnews.go.com/Technology/story?id=1522119.*

Chapter Eight

1. *www.passionatecommitment.com.* (Used by permission.)

2. "Violence and Homosexuality," Family Research Institute, P.O. Box 2091, Washington, DC 20013.

3. *http://www.usatoday.com/news/washington/2006-10-15 -unmarried-households_x.htm?POE=click-refer.*

4. Hannah Brueckner and Peter Bearman, National Longitudinal Study of Adolescent Health, funded by the National Institute of Child Health and Human Development and the Centers for Disease Control and Prevention (April 2005).

5. Ibid.

6. Personal correspondence with Dr. Ross.

7. Robert Rector, "The Effectiveness of Abstinence Education Programs in Reducing Sexual Activity Among Youth," Heritage Foundation, April 8, 2002, *www.heritage.org/Research/ Family/BG1533.cfm.*

Chapter Nine

1. *The Purity Code* audio resource is meant to bring together excellent discussion with your preteen or teen. The topics are relevant, and much of the audio is made up of interviews and dialogue with some of the top authorities who speak to teens and preteens on this subject. There are also a number of discussion starters for older teens in the book *Accept Nothing Less* (available Fall 2008).

JIM BURNS, PhD, founded the ministry HomeWord in 1985 with the goal of bringing help and hope to struggling families. As host of the radio broadcast *HomeWord With Jim Burns*, heard daily in over eight hundred communities, Jim's passion is to build God-honoring families through communicating practical truths that will enable adults and young people alike to live out their Christian faith.

In addition to the radio program, Jim speaks to thousands around the world each year through seminars and conferences. He is also senior director of the HomeWord Center for Youth and Family at Azusa Pacific University, as well as an award-winning author, whose books include *The 10 Building Blocks for a Happy Family* and *Creating an Intimate Marriage*.

Jim and his wife, Cathy, have three grown daughters and live in Southern California.

More Trusted Resources From Family Expert Jim Burns

Painless Parenting Advice

Because kids don't come with a built-in instruction manual, the thought of parenting can leave you feeling overwhelmed and under-prepared. But Jim Burns, host of HomeWord radio broadcast, offers hope—and time-tested advice—by revealing three keys to building a solid parenting foundation.

Confident Parenting by Jim Burns

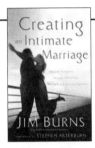

Reset the Emotional Thermostat of Your Marriage

With his candid, laid-back style, Jim Burns, host of HomeWord radio broadcast, shares simple, practical, and thoughtful ways any couple can use to create the intimacy needed in a healthy and loving relationship.

"Jim Burns offers something that will help every marriage become more intimate....Couples need this practical, down-to-earth guide."
—Dr. Henry Cloud, bestselling author of *Boundaries*

Creating an Intimate Marriage by Jim Burns

Small Group/Church DVD Package also available at www.bethanyhouse.com

HOME WORD

WHERE PARENTS GET REAL ANSWERS

Get Equipped with HomeWord...

LISTEN
HomeWord Radio
programs reach over 800 communities nationwide with *HomeWord with Jim Burns* – a daily ½ hour interview feature, *HomeWord Snapshots* – a daily 1 minute family drama, and *HomeWord this Week* – a ½ hour weekend edition of the daily program, and our one-hour program.

CLICK
HomeWord.com
provides advice and resources to millions of visitors each year. A truly interactive website, HomeWord.com provides access to parent newsletter, Q&As, online broadcasts, tip sheets, our online store and more.

READ
HomeWord Resources
parent newsletters, equip families and Churches worldwide with practical Q&As, online broadcasts, tip sheets, our online store and more. Many of these resources are also packaged digitally to meet the needs of today's busy parents.

ATTEND
HomeWord Events
Understanding Your Teenager, Building Healthy Morals & Values, Generation 2 Generation and Refreshing Your Marriage are held in over 100 communities nationwide each year. HomeWord events educate and encourage parents while providing answers to life's most pressing parenting and family questions.

A Ministry with *Jim Burns*

In response to the overwhelming needs of parents and families, Jim Burns founded HomeWord in 1985. HomeWord, a Christian organization, equips and encourages parents, families, and churches worldwide.

Find Out More
Sign up for our FREE daily
e-devotional and parent e-newsletter
at HomeWord.com, or call 800.397.9725.

HomeWord.com

Parent and Family Resources from HomeWord

Parenting Teenagers for Positive Results

This popular resource is designed for small groups and Sunday schools. The kit includes a DVD to begin each of the six sessions featuring a real family situation played out in humorous family vignettes followed by words of wisdom by youth and family expert, Jim Burns, Ph.D., from HomeWord. Each DVD session averages 5 minutes.

The kit contains:
DVD, CD with printable leader's guides and participant guides.

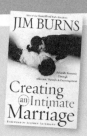

Creating an Intimate Marriage

Jim Burns wants every couple to experience a marriage filled with A.W.E.: affection, warmth, and encouragement. He shows husbands and wives how to make their marriage their priority as they discover ways to repair the past, communicate and resolve conflict, refresh their marriage spiritually, and more!

Confident Parenting

This is a must-have resource for today's family. Let Jim Burns help you to tackle overcrowded lives, negative family patterns, while creating a grace-filled home and raising kids who love God and themselves.

How to Talk to Your Kids About Drugs

Kids can't avoid being exposed to drug use today, some as early as grade school. Packed with practical information and time-proven prevention techniques, this book is a realistic, up-to-date, comprehensive plan for drug-proofing your kids. And if you suspect your kids are already using drugs and alcohol, respected counselor Steve Arterburn and well-known parenting and family expert Jim Burns offer step-by-step advice to get them straight and sober.

Tons of helpful resources for parents and youth.
Visit our online store at www.HomeWord.com
Or call us at 800-397-9725

HOME WORD
WHERE PARENTS GET REAL ANSWERS

Devotionals from Jim Burns
for you and your kids...

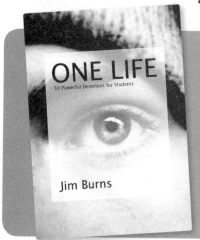

One Life

Your kids only have one life – help them discover the greatest adventure life has to offer! 50 fresh devotional readings that cover many of the major issues of life and faith your kids are wrestling with such as sex, family relationships, trusting God, worry, fatigue and daily surrender. And it's perfect for you and your kids to do together!

Addicted to God

Is your kids' time absorbed by MySpace, text messaging and hanging out at the mall? This devotional will challenge them to adopt thankfulness, make the most of their days and never settle for mediocrity! Fifty days in the Scripture is bound to change your kids' lives forever.

Devotions on the Run

These devotionals are short, simple, and spiritual. They will encourage you to take action in your walk with God. Each study stays in your heart throughout the day, providing direction and clarity when it is most needed.

90 Days Through the New Testament

Downloadable devotional. Author Jim Burns put together a Bible study devotional program for himself to follow, one that would take him through the New Testament in three months. His simple plan was so powerful that he was called to share it with others. A top seller!